Contents

For Jonathan and Hannah

Preface

This book is about what goes on in classrooms as teachers help children to become readers and writers. Throughout the book teachers and children talk about the literacy learning process in an attempt to discover more about literacy in the primary curriculum. Two main areas of enquiry form the focus for analysis:

What is literacy? What does it mean to be literate?
How do we become literate? How is literacy best developed?

After looking at ways of defining and talking about literacy, the book goes on to explore the development of literacy in primary children. Within the context of literacy as 'meaning-making' in a social context, views and practices of teachers and children are explored. Teachers talk about how they came to change their classroom practices and the thinking behind their approach to literacy learning. Children's work is then examined to see how attitudes and behaviours are formed and influenced. The underlying notion within the book is that literacy offers us access to information, ideas, opinions and by creating the potential for reflecting, provides opportunities for making and communicating meaning, and for learning.

An underlying theme of the book is to listen to and observe teachers and children. Its aim is not to prescribe particular 'methods' or to define 'good practice' but rather to explore classroom activity and the literacy learning process in the classroom in relation to learning at home and in the community. As meaning making is central to literacy, so is the search for meaning at the heart of this book: the meaning of literacy in the primary curriculum.

Acknowledgments

I wish to express my sincere and deep gratitude to all those teachers, throughout the country, who gave me access to their classrooms and were so willing to talk with me. My thanks also to the children who let me take their work away and continually interrupt them with my questions, and to the parents who let me intrude into that precious time of the bedtime story. To them all I give my thanks; without them this book would not exist.

I thank Mary-Jane Drummond and Andrew Pollard for their support, encouragement and patience.

Finally I must thank my husband and daughter who tolerated so much during the writing process; their love and support came just at the right moments.

The Primary Curriculum Series

This innovative series promotes reflective teaching and active forms of pupil learning. The books explore the implications of these commitments for curriculum and curriculum-related issues.

The argument of each book flows in, around and among a variety of case studies of classroom practice, introducing them, probing, analysing, and teasing out their implications before moving on to the next stage of the argument. The case study material varies in source and form – children's work, teachers' work, diary entries, drawings, poetry, literature, interviews. The vitality and richness of primary school practice are conveyed, together with the teacher expertise on which these qualities are based.

Introduction

What is literacy?

The teaching of reading and writing is a subject which continually has a high profile in the media and in the minds of the general public. Headlines proclaim that standards are falling and so enquiries are set up and teaching approaches investigated. However, literacy is very rarely carefully defined in these debates; as a result, words are used which may have different meanings to different people and the argument becomes emotive and without cohesion.

It seems to me that no discussion or analysis of literacy learning can take place without reference to precise historical and cultural contexts. The first two questions raised by this book: *What is literacy? What does it mean to be literate?* depend for their answers on particular contexts. It must be that the answers will vary from culture to culture, and from period to period.

Parents attending a primary school parents' evening were asked for their definitions of reading and writing. Communication featured prominently in both definitions. Writing was seen predominantly as being able to communicate and to record ideas and information. Reading was also seen as a means of communication but, in addition, a great variety of ideas was introduced with words such as 'decoding', 'learning the sounds', 'deciphering', 'translation', 'enjoyment' and 'making sense'. One appealing definition was that reading is 'making sense out of 26 variable characters'.

Such an activity is of little use if one is searching for a single definition of literacy, other than showing that there are as many views of literacy as there are people. A common-sense, simplistic definition of literacy is that it concerns all those activities that are to do with the written word. Modern day society is full of print; successful functioning in the world requires a high degree of literacy competence. However, the phenomenon 'literacy' or the state of being 'literate' has much broader connotations than just being able to read and write, in the sense of possessing the necessary skills.

Some see becoming literate as concerned with gaining familiarity with the great works of literature of our cultural heritage; this view has some historical precedents. For many years literacy was seen as the privilege of the élite. Possession of literacy was highly valued and gave the owner status in society. Books were expensive and could only be afforded by the rich. The acquisition of literacy was very closely bound up with religious faith; the sanctity of the 'Word' could only be freely available to the masses through the mediation of the literate hierarchy. This view of literacy as some elevated phenomenon contrasts with the view of literacy as a skill which enables everyone to operate within the society of which one is a part. It was only with the development of printing technology that language in its written forms became gradually more available to the 'masses' and more necessary for the daily business of living.

The concept of 'functional literacy' has been adopted in many considerations of literacy standards. In 1962 UNESCO stated that,

> A person is literate when he has acquired the essential knowledge and skills which enable him to engage in all those activities in which literacy is required for effective functioning in his group or community. (Oxenham, 1980, p. 87)

There are several drawbacks to this definition. First, it takes no account of the role of literacy as an agent of change. It must surely be agreed that the development of literacy, when viewed historically over time and within an individual, can be seen as a process of change and evolution. Graff (1987 p.71) asserts that the epistemological considerations about literacy are, for the most part, evolutionary ones. The development of literacy must be connected with the development of a society and the structures of power and control.

Freire (1970) argued that literacy is a means of social control; it is only when people are able to read that those in power are able to feed them with propaganda and set out rules and regulations. There is a counter argument, however, that literacy gives people freedom and the ability to fight against the establishment.

Whatever perspective is adopted, one can see that the UNESCO definition of functional literacy is deficient in failing to consider the potential of literacy for change.

Second, the UNESCO definition fails to take into account the cultural definition of literacy. The question of what is seen to be 'effective functioning' within a community and who defines this effectiveness is an important one in terms of assessment of literacy standards. About 20 years ago a reading age of about nine to ten was required to read the *Daily Mirror* but today a reading age of 14 to 15 is needed to read the same paper. Is this a sign of rising or falling standards?

Literacy is much more than the 'simple' acts of reading and writing; it involves notions of power, of culture and community and of social learning. To understand literacy, it is necessary to explore all these areas and see how the use of print is part of the social heritage of a community.

Standards – rising or falling?

Since the publication of *Sponsored Reading Failure* (1990) Martin Turner's report describing an alleged dramatic decline in reading standards, the debate has raged fiercely. To read the headlines in the popular press one would imagine that we are a nation of illiterates, unable to read, write or spell. Evidence from elsewhere, however, suggests that this is not necessarily so. The H.M.I. survey of primary schools in 1990 focussed particularly on reading. In their published report (HMSO 1990) the Inspectorate also drew on evidence from another 3000 visits to schools made after September 1989. They found that standards of reading were satisfactory or better than satisfactory in 80% of the schools visited and that in 30% standards could be described as high. They also found that no single method of teaching reading dominated. Twenty percent of schools needed 'urgent attention' because of poor reading standards. Putting aside the question of what counts as good or poor standards, this proportion of schools where the teaching of reading is deemed to need attention may not be thought acceptable. Yet it is far from the popular view of many pupils leaving school unable to read at all, because their teachers adopted 'trendy' methods and left them to soak up reading for themselves.

Lake (1991) takes this argument one stage further and asks what could be the causes of these reading failures and if they can really be attributed to the teaching methods employed. Lake looked at one specific geographical area over 12 years and identified a slight but consistent drop in reading standards between 1985 and 1989, with a small rise in 1990. From his data Lake feels that there was an increase in the proportion of 'slow starters' over the 12 years and that the effect of the school's catchment area was a more significant influence than change or continuity of reading policy. The main feature of this deterioration was the extent of the support children had from home.

A report by NFER (1992) seems to support this view. This indicates a decline in reading standards between 1987 and 1991, but also reveals that considerable differences existed between geographical areas. The greatest decline was found in areas where there was an increase in child poverty and changing patterns in family life.

Whose literacy?

Meek (1991) defines literacy as 'being in control' and it is true that fully literate children have the potential to control themselves and their environment, through access to information, ideas, opinions: such is the power of literacy that teaching it could be defined as 'empowerment'. Willinsky (1990) argues that the proponents of what he describes as the 'new literacy' have failed to live up to the social and political implications of this way of thinking. It is, he says, not just a new way of teaching, but a new way of thinking with all the implications that brings.

On 10 November 1991 the leader of *The Mail On Sunday* launched an attack on 'progressive' teaching methods. Applauding the proposal to introduce the teaching of grammar and 'formal teaching methods' in English, the article said that children would now receive, 'an education where they are taught the basics; an education which equips them for the adult world; an education which tests and challenges them.'

The contrast between this and the view expressed by Willinsky is interesting. On the one hand there is a view of literacy as giving learners the power to create their own meanings, in which 'response becomes connection' within a community of readers; literacy is seen as a way of enabling and empowering people. On the other hand, the teaching of basic skills, using the methods of several decades ago, where literacy is seen as a value-free skill, is considered the way forward. The political implications of this are enormous, despite the belief of Mona McKee (*Times Educational Supplement* July 1992) that reading is not a political activity. However, writing in *The Observer* on 22 September 1991 Barry Hugill says,

> To take control of the curriculum is the ultimate political act. Politics is about power and about ideas. By limiting access to ideas ... government strengthens the status quo.

In the promotion of a literacy in schools which seeks not only to maintain the status quo but to revert to the understandings of earlier times, the power of thought and ideas is taken under central control.

Gee (1990) argues that all behaviour take place within specific discourses, that there are ways of behaving and interacting appropriate to particular roles as recognised by specific groups of people. In this view, literacy, like any other behaviour, is a socially constructed activity. Gee puts it this way:

> There is no such thing as 'reading' or 'writing', only reading or writing *something* (a text of certain type) in a certain way with certain values, while at least appearing to think and feel in certain ways. (p. xvii)

Taken further, it can be argued that literacy plays a large part in creating the reality within which it operates. It is a chicken and egg situation; each has a part in the construction of the other.

Anderson et al (1984) use and define the term 'literacy events' as, 'any action sequence, involving one or more persons, in which the production and/or comprehension of print plays a role'. (p.59). They go on to identify two types of literacy events. First, reading events are those where a graphically encoded message is comprehended. Second, writing events are where an individual produces those graphic signs, encoding spoken language.

The term 'literacy event' has echoes with the term 'speech event' used by Hymes (1972). Speech events occur in social contexts and are governed by particular rules. Likewise, literacy events are not isolated fragments of activity but are embedded in socially assembled transactions. On the basis of their research, Anderson and Stokes (1984) argue that book reading, story time and other experiences related to books are not the only forms of literacy experience but are a small proportion of the ways in which print can be experienced. They constructed an analytic system of 'domains of literacy', including cinema and television, and found that there was a link between the types of literacy material used and the actions constructed around them in terms of both the content and the text structure. They concluded that literacy is influenced largely by social institutions and not cultural membership. Many families engaged in literate behaviour within the domains of daily living and entertainment which, because of the emphasis in classrooms on particular types of behaviour, for example, story reading and writing, were not fully acknowledged within the culture of a school. Most 'literacy events' are deeply embedded in the social context in which they take place.

Literacy in the culture of home and school

Let us move this argument into the classroom and suppose that the teaching of literacy is done through simple texts, with a controlled vocabulary, and phonically consistent words, meted out to the learners a few at a time. In this sort of classroom learning is constructed as a predictable, linear, hierarchical process and there is an implicit 'deficit theory' of children's understandings. This construction of the world will set constraints on the relationships between teacher and pupil, and will affect both the physical and social environment of the classroom and the resources and methods employed. A classroom where children actively engage with print, creating meanings of their own, reading and writing for themselves with adults acting as guides and mentors, will be the site of a completely differently constructed reality.

Schiefflin and Cochran-Smith (1984) examined the literacy learning of pre-school children in a school orientated community. They found that both in the home and in nursery school the context of literacy events was hardly ever that of instruction. Instead, literacy events were embedded within the routine social interactions of adults and children. Within these social contexts, adults used print to acknowledge, reflect and give credibility to the children's feelings. The researchers concluded that what was important was not so much being surrounded by print but being surrounded by adults who used print because of its effectiveness. However, the children were not passive observers in these literacy events. As in the development of oral language, adults used literacy events to meet perceived or anticipated needs of the children. Thus the children could interact with print although they did not have the skills of decoding and encoding.

This compares with the findings of the major study of children's language development carried out by Wells and his group (1981). He sees literacy as 'the full exploitation of the meanings encoded in language' (p. 266). He identifies three major phases in a child's linguistic development. First a young child discovers language as s/he realises that sounds serve functions within specific social contexts. Secondly, the child goes through a process of consolidation and diversification, and, as competence increases, the child absorbs the language assumptions and behaviour of the cultural group. Thirdly, a child begins to be able to use language to reflect on experience and thus to construct her/his own interpretation of others' behaviours. It is the acquisition of literacy, according to Wells, which supports this third stage of development. In their story reading adults were seen as modelling the behaviour of fluent readers, so enabling children to bring meaning to the text and take meaning from it. In this way the children learned to become active participants in the text. Wells sees literacy in terms of its meanings; literate behaviour is about transmitting meanings within a social context.

Cook-Gumperz (1986) takes up the idea that literate behaviour does not depend on the acquisition of decoding and encoding skills. She describes literacy as a 'socially constructed phenomenon' which is formed through interactions in a variety of contexts. Therefore literacy could be said not to be constructed or recreated as it is encountered in different literacy events.

This construction of literacy, however, must take place within the social rules of the context; much literacy learning is about coming to an understanding of these rules. Cook-Gumperz (1978) describes the 'situated meaning' of verbal messages and says that verbal behaviour must meet the adult criteria of contextually relevant and appropriate speech. This brings us to the notion of what counts as valid learning.

The understanding of literacy with which children come to school will reflect the literacy which has been created in their home and local environment. This point is aptly illustrated by the work of Shirley Brice Heath (1983), in which the patterns of literacy learning within different communities are explored. In one community, Trackton, reading was nearly always set in a context of immediate action. Children learned from a very young age to have expectations of print and that the meanings of the written word come about through the negotiation of the group, as the oral tradition played a large part in the literate life of the community. Books were not common in these homes and reading came from their daily life and social interactions. For Trackton children, reading was 'reading to learn what they need to know before they go to school to be successful in their community' (p. 233). In other words, literate behaviour is always connected with action.

In another community, Roadville, by contrast, reading was a highly-valued activity and books played an important and significant part in the lives of young children. From the bedtime story to blocks marked with letters of the alphabet to writing workbooks, literacy was seen as an absolute means of expression which is not open to negotiation. The relationship between these two 'definitions' of literacy and the view which was valued in school will be considered later. It is enough for now to remind ourselves that children come to school with very different experiences of, expectations of and ways of approaching literate behaviour.

Scribner and Cole (1981) worked among the Vai people in Liberia and concluded that the way in which literacy is learned has a major influence on the cognitive consequences of literacy understandings and the ways in which competencies are put to use. The work of Scribner and Cole made an attempt to distinguish between schooling and literacy and this distinction is an important one in any consideration of how children become literate. We need to consider the definitions of literacy which operate in school and in the world of the child outside school, for it may well be that the two differ in some essential aspects. Without an understanding of the two different perspectives any analysis of literacy learr.'ng will fall short of the truth. The notion of literacy as a socially constructed phenomenon influences our analysis and response to current concerns about and pressures on literacy learning.

Schooling and literacy

Bloome (1986) views classrooms as communities, thus recognising the importance of the social nature of classroom activity. He describes his perspective as an 'interactive sociolinguistic' one. The community of a classroom is, according to Bloome, constructed, maintained and re-constructed through language. In examining this process of construction he attempts to come closer to an understanding of the relationship between literacy and schooling. He believes that there is an inherent link between the nature of schooling and the development of literacy understandings.

Bloome identifies three levels of social group within the community of a classroom: teacher and class, teacher and individual pupil and peer-peer. For Bloome, 'any group of people who are somehow engaged in doing an activity constitutes a social group' (p. 3). There is a constant process of establishment and maintenance of social groups within a classroom in the norms established for interacting with other members, in the social and other goals held in common by members and in the continuous display of membership by members. Influences on the nature of such social groups are the development of classroom communicative competence and the nature of academic work within a classroom. The actual work which is done may not be that which was planned or intended by the teacher. Bloome believes that the nature of a classroom as a community will influence the extent to which external frameworks for understanding literacy are brought into the classroom. The importance for Bloome of understanding classroom 'procedural displays' is in the light this throws on the nature of classroom literacy.

In a way similar to that of Heath, emphasis is placed on the definition of literacy within a community and the process of socialisation through which children learn literacy. The focus of examining classroom literacy and the factors influencing it are widening. Definitions of literacy must take into account the context within which literacy events occur and the interactive processes which are part of a particular literacy event.

Smith (1983) also views literacy as a socio-cultural phenomenon and says that, 'Each school develops its own culture (or subculture) of literacy' (p. 174). It could also be argued that within a school each class develops its own culture of literacy. For if one is to say, as Smith does, that reading and writing are adaptive processes, then within a social context, individual members of a social group bring their own perspectives, engage in their own processes of construction and negotiation and adopt their own literacy behaviours. The nature of literacy within a classroom could be a result of all these individual literacies and be created through processes of negotiation and adaptation.

Langer (1986) broadens the definition of literacy even further and makes a distinction between literacy as an act of reading and writing, and literacy as a way of thinking and speaking. She argues that literacy involves special uses of language; these and the cognitive behaviours they invoke need not necessarily be encoded in print. A community modifies its literate behaviours to meet changing needs of society. This understanding of literacy has important implications for classroom literacy learning. Learning is, in this perspective, based on a process of social cooperation, and classroom literacy events will encourage children to become flexible and independent thinkers, involved in conscious action on their own literacy understandings.

The meaning of literacy

Our discussion on the nature of literacy has moved from a description of the individual bringing knowledge and experience to a text in order to make sense of it (Smith 1978, Goodman 1978) to a description of literacy as a way of thinking and literacy learning as a process of social cooperation. Halliday (1978) brings the context into focus and in seeing language as *learning how to mean* within a context, identifies the learning process as a social one. Heath's work (1983) forms a watershed in our understanding of literacy learning. Literacy is seen as culture specific, and literacy learning occurs within a particular culture. Bloome (1986) and Smith (1983) transferred this notion to the classroom, which is another culture with its own definitions of literacy. Literacy learning has come to be seen as an interactive, adaptive and cooperative process.

Bruner and Haste (1987) re-emphasise the importance of the relationship between the individual and the social. The child, in learning literacy within a classroom, needs to integrate his/her own needs, strategies and interpretations with those significant others around him/her. There are links here with Vygotsky's view (1962) that children first acquire concepts externally, in dialogue, and then internally, to elaborate and differentiate thought. Thus children's developing concepts are dependent on the concepts expressed within their particular culture. This links with the work of Berger and Luckman (1966) in describing the child's 'social construction of reality' where meanings and concepts are reproduced and modified through language. So the emphasis is placed on interaction for transmission of meanings and the

... enactment of shared interpretations and common symbolic representations. Such social facts reflect and also generate the framework within which individual experience is interpreted. (p. 6)

The Piagetian view of the solitary child is replaced by a view of a child engaged in a collaborative problem-solving process. Therefore, any exploration or discussion of classroom literacy learning needs to look at children in a normal social situation as they attempt to make sense of the literacy within that culture and construct their own understandings.

It is this understanding which underpins the case studies and the analysis of them in the rest of this book. Children are described engaged in a variety of literacy events which are all seen as attempts to 'make meaning'. As the children make their own meanings from the literacy culture in which they find themselves, the analysis attempts to make meaning of the literacy processes that are taking place. The whole book is a search for meaning at many different levels and in many different ways; as the worlds of classroom literacies are entered so the 'meaning makers' engage in the process of construction. I hope that as reader and writer make meaning some clarification and understanding are found.

Conclusion

Within the understanding of literacy arrived at in this introductory chapter, the book explores approaches to literacy learning within several classrooms in different primary schools. The connection between what is happening and what is being learned is an ongoing theme. By listening to teachers and children, and by observing their literacy behaviours, I hope to identify some of the dilemmas faced by teachers today and to explore how the process of becoming literate can be facilitated within classrooms.

The questions that have been raised in this introduction: *What is literacy?* and *How is literacy best developed?* form the basis for the observations and analyses in the rest of the book. In exploring teachers' accounts of their practices and looking at literacy behaviours of children – from the beginners to older primary children – I hope to come to some understanding of literacy in these primary schools. I attempt to 'make meaning' of the process of literacy learning and hope that for the readers the observations and analyses will help their own meaning making.

CHAPTER ONE

Approaches to Literacy

Introduction

This chapter begins with an outline of different approaches to literacy and the understanding of the child as a learner implicit in each approach. These different views are put into the context of the present debate about 'standards' and related to what actually goes on in classrooms.

One teacher then gives an account of how she considered her approach to writing and embarked on the process of change. The factors influencing this process are highlighted and discussed so that other teachers may be helped as they interrogate their own practice.

Views of learning

There can be no doubt that literacy learning is considered to be one of the prime areas of importance in primary schools today and that it is often used as the touchstone for assessing a 'good' school. The issue of standards of literacy teaching and thus of literacy learning has been in the forefront of recent debate and teachers are under pressure to produce good results that will account for the approach they have chosen to adopt.

For many years questions were rarely asked about the nature of classroom literacy and how children can best be enabled to learn to read and write. It was considered enough to have chosen a scheme and to work through it, supplementing the books with art and craft activities, writing and games to reinforce the reading materials. Then the 'real books' movement came to influence many teachers and the rigid structure of the reading scheme was questioned. Researchers began to focus on the processes of reading and writing and to explore what it is that facilitates the development of literacy both in those who succeed early (Clark 1976) and in those who have failed (Meek 1983). From this work much emphasis was placed on the resources used. The work of Jill Bennett (1982) exercised a great influence on many teachers. Barrie Wade (1982) in his well-known article illustrating the literary and linguistic paucity of reading books led many teachers to look more closely at the books they were using in their classrooms. Some teachers allowed children free access to a range of 'real' books. Reactions to this movement ranged from full support to hostile opposition; words and phrases like 'structure', 'learning by osmosis' and 'no teaching' were thrown into the air.

The work of the Goodmans (1978) and Smith (1983) did much to help teachers understand literacy learning as a process and to evaluate what it is that best enables children to become competent and effective within that process. K. Goodman (1978) described the interaction between reader and writer as a 'psycholinguistic guessing game'; he showed us how in literacy learning the child is learning how to mean. The emphasis is on the way in which individual children construct meaning from a text. As children engage in literacy events within their culture, they form, test and reformulate hypotheses about the functions and forms of written language. The vast majority of young children begin school with some experience and understanding of these forms and functions; but this understanding is sometimes not fully exploited. Early literacy experiences in the classroom are sometimes simplified to such an extent that the written materials available do not reflect the full complexity of written language.

Smith (1983) argues against the tendency of cognitive psychologists to see the brain as an information processing device. Viewed from this perspective, literacy learning is seen as stimulus-response learning, with the emphasis on decoding and graphophonic correspondence. Smith argues that learning is a creative process and that literacy learning is a process of creating worlds, an argument he describes as a constructivist one. For Smith, reading involves the use of a quantity of non-visual information; a reader is engaged in anticipating meaning through the process of making sense of print using syntactic and semantic as well as graphophonic cues. Literacy learning, according to Smith, comes about as children see language demonstrated in a purposeful way, as a way of expressing meaning.

Both Smith and Goodman stress the similarities between oral

language learning and written language learning, arguing that both require the same sort of cognitive action. This perspective on the nature of classroom literacy has implications for the environment that teachers create to facilitate literacy learning. Smith's view of learning as a creative process means that children must be given the opportunity to engage in this process. The classroom environment and the activities provided must be meaningful, relevant and purposeful. Furthermore, teachers who adopt the psycholinguistic perspective on early literacy, take a very positive view of young children as literacy learners. Work on children's errors or miscues in reading (Clay 1982, Goodman 1979) shows children engaged in a sense-making activity as they seek a 'reduction in uncertainty' (Smith 1978).

The psycholinguistic view of literacy learning has been useful in the emphasis it has placed on the competence of young literacy learners and in the support it has given to teachers who recognise that literacy learning cannot be simplified to a 'single set of stepping stones from confusion to clarity' and feel that 'an important way for many learners will be to build their own bridges from their own knowledge of language and of reading as a pleasure-giving pursuit.' (Wade 1990).

Many teachers were pleased that the National Curriculum documentation for English seemed to support this view of the complex nature of literacy learning. The Cox Report (1988) stated that 'Teachers should recognise that reading is a complex but unitary process and not a set of skills which can be taught separately in turn and, ultimately, bolted together' (9.7). The curriculum in English for Key Stage 1 can be said to reflect the complexity of literacy learning as it is now understood. The Programmes of Study certainly reflect the cyclical nature of this learning and the importance of the social context. Contexts are specified but not a single or simple teaching approach. Some teachers saw this as an opportunity to select particular phrases from the documents which supported their own individual classroom approaches.

As teachers began to explore the complex nature of literacy learning and to understand the rich literacy competencies with which children arrive at school, the importance of the social context of their learning came to the fore. The work of Brice Heath (1983) showed how children bring different expectations and different experiences of literacy to school, determined by their social community. These differences are not of degree but rather of kind. The emphasis in Heath's work moves from the individual learning literacy to the individual as a member of a community that socialises the individual into its own literate behaviours and values. The implications of this emphasis for classroom practice will be considered further in the next chapter, suffice it for now to say that the social dimension of the literacy environment of the classroom became an important issue of consideration for many teachers.

In the middle of this development of understanding about the process of literacy learning came the onslaught on 'standards'. Teachers were once more thrown into confusion about the 'best' approach to literacy learning.

On 29 June 1990 the *Daily Telegraph* led with a story about appalling literacy standards and the claim that the nation's teachers were letting down the children in their care. Martin Turner, educational psychologist, subsequently published his pamphlet *Sponsored Reading Failure* (1990). The evidence on which Turner's claims were based was not made clear and so it was difficult for teachers to argue against or even evaluate them. However, the media soon took up the clarion call and the general public was warned against those 'trendy teachers' who were responsible for the decline in standards. The issue was immediately polarised into a 'real books – it will all happen anyway' approach and a 'we must have a structure and teach each stage thoroughly' approach.

What are the prevalent approaches to literacy in schools? When *Child Education* magazine carried out a survey in 1991 it found that teachers are much more eclectic than commonly portrayed in the popular press. There is evidence that teachers are thinking about the issues and weighing them up in the context of their own classrooms, choosing from a variety of approaches and using the best of each. In fact an association known as 'Balance' was set up in 1990 to support this viewpoint. As Wade (1990) says 'The facts about how individual children learn to read cannot be contained in one single theory.' It is unlikely that one single approach to teaching reading could ever be appropriate.

In an *Observer* special report (22.9.91) Professor Ted Wragg wrote about the 'conflict that doesn't exist' arguing that most teachers use a variety of approaches. His argument was endorsed by the survey of the teaching of reading in primary schools carried out by Her Majesty's Inspectorate (1991). They found that only five percent of primary teachers used an exclusively 'real books' approach and only three percent a totally phonics approach. The majority use a variety of approaches, relating to the needs of the children and the context in which they are working. They will use, for example, a core scheme supported by a variety of other books both from schemes and 'real' books; they will teach phonics and will ensure that the children develop a sight vocabulary of key words as well as possessing strategies for tackling unknown words. HMI found that the poorest reading achievement was found in classrooms where only one approach was used.

These findings seem to indicate that teachers are continually reflecting on literacy learning in their classrooms. They examine pedagogy, resources and contexts, asking questions to determine what is best for their children. Most teachers do not casually adopt what seems to be the latest fashion or the newest published scheme but carefully consider issues relating them to their experience and the context in which they work.

An account of change

The remainder of this chapter will consider the process through which one teacher went as she reflected on the literacy learning of the children in her class. I worked with Sue in her classroom in the year 1987-8; she wrote an account of her change of approach for a course on early literacy in which she participated several months later. The extracts given here are taken from that account.

Sue was focussing on the teaching of writing in her reception class. The school was a nursery/infant school in an old industrial area of a large city. It consisted of four parallel nursery classes and three infant classes. Sue's class was the reception class of 20 children, with a teacher (Sue) and a nursery nurse working full-time in the classroom. All the children had been in the nursery and came into the reception class when they were five. We will look at what Sue herself said about the implementation of change and consider the implications of her remarks. She began by saying:

There has to be a good reason for change and clear evidence made available to all involved in it.

At first sight this is a sound statement, which makes good sense; and yet it leads itself to further investigation. It is useful to pause and ask ourselves questions before we move on.

1 What might be deemed a good reason for change? Teachers have given many reasons for changing their practice; the following list is by no means comprehensive:

- I read about it in a magazine.
- A new head told me to change.
- My colleague did it this way and it seemed to work for her.
- I've been on an inservice course.
- The books were getting tatty and needed replacing anyway.
- Nothing else seemed to work with these children.
- I was in a rut and felt like a change.

All of these might be classed as 'good reasons'. Yet are they sufficient in themselves for changes in approach? Who or what determines the validity of a reason for change? And why?

It is important as well to remember the significance of the context in determining what changes might be valid and acceptable to particular teachers. This context includes the influence of media reports, parental pressure, the policy of the local authority and of other schools in the neighbourhood and, perhaps most importantly, the teacher's own understanding of the children in her class.

2 'Clear evidence' is cited as a criterion for change. Where do most teachers get their evidence from? Inservice courses, discussions with colleagues and the work involved in drawing up curriculum policy statements are all sources of information about current thinking and practice. Classroom teachers will evaluate new information against their own professional judgement, their experience and the context within which they work. It is the practice of reflective pedagogy (Pollard and Tann 1987) which enables teachers to evaluate as fully as possible all evidence available to them.

3 The final element given in this teacher's description of the process of change is the people involved in that change. She states that all the reasons for change must be seen to be good by them and that clear evidence must be available to them. Who are these people and are the reasons and evidence the same for all of them?

a) *The teachers* How is change seen by the whole staff of a school? The days when an individual teacher could shut his or her classroom door and do what s/he alone saw fit are long past; negotiation is now a much more common feature of staff discussion in determining curriculum policy. Within these negotiations it

becomes clear that there are as many 'good' reasons for not chang-
ing as there are for change:
- I've always done it this way.
- We've already got the resources.
- The children like it.
- It's only a passing fashion.
- It won't work with children like these.
- The parents are happy with how we do things.

Who is to say which reasons and which sources of evidence are
more valid?

b) *The children* It is a basic premise of child-centred education that
we start where the children are and provide experiences that will
develop and extend their learning. Clay (1972, 1975, 1982) and
Goodman (1976, 1980) are among those who have stressed the
importance of teachers making detailed observations of children's
literacy learning behaviours. It is these observations that inform
the planning of worthwhile literacy events and contexts. Paley's
(1981, 1986) vivid narrative accounts of children's responses to
classroom activities and behaviours show how observation is the
basis of good practice. A teacher needs to know where children are
in order to take them on in an appropriate way. Vygotsky's notion
of the 'zone of proximal development' is central here in defining
children's conceptual development and understanding. Bruner
and Haste (1987) re-emphasise the importance of the relationship
between individuals and their social context. The Piagetian view of
the solitary child (one which could be said to be reflected in the
work of Smith and Goodman) is replaced by a view of children
engaged in a collaborative problem-solving process, making sense
of the situation in which they find themselves and constructing
their own understandings. The Primary Language Record (1989) is
an excellent, if demanding, way of organising and recording observations of these essentially social learners.

c) *The parents* 'Accountability' seems to be the key word of the
nineties and teachers are increasingly being required to explain
their approaches and 'results' to parents. The Parents' Charter
(D.E.S. 1991) does much to support parents' rights to know about
and determine their child's education, but does little to establish
and support teachers' professional judgement and understanding.

Teachers need to be able to articulate clearly the basis for their decisions in the classroom and to give reasoned accounts of their practice. Assessment of results is a more complex issue, particularly when related to literacy learning. Parents, in the past, were given explanations and accounts by teachers that no longer seem appropriate. 'Progress' was defined as an uncomplicated journey from Book 1 through to Book 10 of a published reading scheme, rather than a process of developing a range of different strategies for understanding written language. Progress and results are much easier to describe when literacy learning is defined in terms of a linear development rather than in a spiral or cyclical form. This conflict is reflected in the relationship between the National Curriculum Programmes of Study and Statements of Attainment. The former reflect the complex nature of literacy learning and the latter attempt to put all of this complexity into a linear structure. The results include some rather odd ordering and a vast range of understanding, summed up in a very short statement. As Dombey (1991) says, '... a simple linear structure has been imposed on a vastly complex sphere of learning in which children do not develop in a simple linear way' (p.44). The reporting of results and the way teachers talk about their teaching are complex issues.

All teachers reflecting on their own classroom practice soon come to realise that any change will extend further than their own classroom walls. Sue's account of her change of approach goes on to say,

Previously my concern had been to change children's attitudes to writing. Once I had gained success in doing this the emphasis changed from influencing children to influencing colleagues.

It is clear that for Sue, the move was from classroom practice to school policy. Sue began by interrogating her own approach and changing that; she then went on, in her role as English curriculum coordinator, to interrogate and change the approaches of her colleagues and the whole school policy. Teachers must ask themselves if this is the right way – what if other members of staff are not convinced and do not want to change?

Consider the school in which each member of staff works according to his or her own beliefs. A reception teacher might well adopt an 'emergent' approach. There will be times of class, group and individual book sharing; children will be encouraged to behave as readers and writers and their literacy behaviours will be accepted and valued as such. Through shared reading and writing, the use of the children's own writing and of familiar stories, and stories from a scheme such as *Letterland* (Wendon 1986) the children will be enabled to use a variety of strategies to make sense of text.

These imaginary children might then move into a Year 1 classroom where the teacher adopts a linear approach to literacy learning. A reading scheme with a graded vocabulary is introduced, the children are given isolated printed words in a tin to take and learn at home and progress is assessed by steady movement through the scheme based on daily reading aloud to the teacher and instant sight recognition of each word in the graded vocabulary. When writing the children dictate simple sentences to the teacher about the picture they have just drawn and then trace over or copy underneath the teacher's writing.

In Year 2 the same published scheme is still used but is extended by a wide variety of books which the children are encouraged to discuss and read with each other and their parents, as well as at school. When writing, emphasis is on content as well as presentation and children's own attempts at spelling are valued and used as a basis for further learning.

It is clear that within such a school it is the children from whom change and adaptability are required. One must ask the question – how far is any teacher justified in following his or her convictions if these do not fit in with the rest of the school? The importance of social interaction in the process of literacy learning within the classroom has already been identified. The whole school environment is also a social context in which issues of negotiation and control are vital. Hargreaves and Pollard (1972, 1985) have shown how the development of a working consensus is an essential element of whole school development. It could well be that within the establishment of a 'working consensus' compromise is another important ingredient.

Sue's account of the process of change that took place within her classroom is divided into three sections: past, present and future. I shall look at each section in turn and in the analysis attempt to come to some understanding of the questions the teacher asked herself of her own practice and so suggest to others a framework for a similar enquiry.

The past

I was using a traditional method of teaching children to write.
This entailed:
1 tracing over my writing, using the children's own writing;
2 copying underneath;
3 transferring to a copybook, and finally
4 using an individual dictionary.

Occasionally they made their own books but this and other divergences were time-consuming, particularly as I placed emphasis upon correct letter formation and good presentation.

All the children had been through our nursery where natural experiences are more readily accepted, although at this time there was no emphasis placed upon literacy and each teacher 'did his own thing'. Instead of continuing with this natural progression, I seemed to be giving these reception class children a set of rules to follow in order to learn to write 'properly'. I remember feeling quite cross if the children were still writing their names using block capitals by the time they reached my class!

Whilst the children enjoyed reading it was obvious they did not feel the same way about writing.

I was becoming increasingly frustrated and could not see a way out until by a number of strange coincidences my literacy awakening and rebirth began! I will try to explain.

A close friend and colleague teaching fourth year juniors had been invited to sit on a panel with other teachers to look at writing in the junior school, with a view to publishing a manual which would help other teachers. They were looking closely at something called the 'National Writing Project'. I was fascinated with the information she fed me from their discussions. All the time I was thinking that infants could adopt this approach, indeed were already carrying out certain aspects like re-drafting, editing and publishing their own writing.

I was later informed that an infant panel had been set up and some schools were already trying out a new way of writing. I remember my feelings of excitement and I was anxious to gather together as much information as possible.

At this time a tutor from the college was carrying out some personal research into literacy and had asked if she could work at our school. Her work involved the study of a group of children from the nursery into the reception class.

At a time of uncertainty on my part I welcomed her presence in my classroom. Perhaps she would be able to help. She was an encourager and her presence was to prove invaluable.

As I explored new literacy areas with the children she pointed out certain aspects for me to think about and possibly to try out. 'Have you thought about just letting the children write unaided?' This was a major consideration! At first the children's presentations seemed messy and careless. Letting go of my high expectations with regard to presentation was difficult.

I had the full support of my headteacher, who felt, like me, that this natural approach to writing was more than a passing fashion.

During the Summer Term I launched the emergent approach to writing in my classroom with just a pilot group of children.

This proved unsatisfactory as the children were confused – some were writing one way, others were allowed to do it in a different way. So by the Autumn Term I felt brave enough to launch the emergent approach to writing within the whole classroom.

I have never looked back.

It seems that four main influences on the beginnings of change can be identified from Sue's account:

1 Colleagues
2 Research
3 Reflection
4 Reading

I shall examine each of these more closely.

1. *Colleagues*

Here we can see the importance of a forum in which teachers can share ideas, both within and between schools. One beneficial side effect of the introduction of the National Curriculum has been that teachers have had to sit down and discuss what they mean by particular statements of attainment. It soon became evident in many schools during the agreement trials that took place during the early implementation of the National Curriculum, that frequently teachers were using the same words to describe different ideas or concepts. As staff groups attempted to clarify issues, a whole-school understanding of literacy emerged. The importance of this for children's literacy learning has already been raised. Throughout their school careers children become members of many different classrooms. In many primary schools, while these classrooms may be influenced by the wider context of the school, each classroom in itself is a unique socio-cultural setting. Within each classroom different relationships and interaction patterns are established, different expectations of behaviours and responses are laid down and there are different resources, organisational patterns and survival strategies adopted by the members of the class. A young child moves through school encountering these differences both within and between classes. How does s/he make sense of this? It must be the responsibility of a school staff to create a consistent approach to literacy, changing and adapting approaches to fit their particular context. However, there must be some constants which are based on our understanding of children's learning in general and of literacy learning in particular. What are these?

Dombey (1991) outlines eight lessons which she considers we have learned in the last 20 years:

> 1 Readers engage in a complex, multi-level process, involving knowledge of sound-symbol relations, spelling patterns, vocabulary, sentence structures, propositional meanings and realms of meaning beyond individual propositions.
>
> 2 Literacy learning is not to be simply and straightforwardly equated with teaching in school.
>
> 3 Literacy learning is an active process driven and shaped by the learner's intentions.
>
> 4 Literacy learning operates most characteristically on a number of different linguistic levels simultaneously; it is not made easier by being broken down into apparently simpler elements, which are then taught separately.
>
> 5 Children vary in the amount of direct teaching they need, but all children do much of their literacy learning 'tacitly', implicitly.
>
> 6 There are many important literacy lessons that only powerful texts can teach.
>
> 7 Literacy is laden with the values of the social context which both surrounds it and is shaped by it.
>
> 8 There is no substitute for watching how, when, where and why children go about the business of reading and writing.

2. *Research*

The word research sometimes suggests an academic activity, pursued by distant professors, uninvolved in everyday realities; but research that influences teachers' practice is rather different. Teachers' understanding of children's learning comes from constant observation and questioning of their behaviour. This observation and questioning is their form of research. It is true for teachers as for many other professionals that past experience creates present understandings. A teacher who is skilled in observing and analysing children's learning behaviours will build up an expert knowledge of child development founded on first-hand classroom experiences. Continual enquiry and reflection will serve to build up a picture of the literacy which exists within a particular classroom. As members of a school staff discuss their questions and observations, commonalities can be identified and established and a vocabulary will emerge for talking about literacy learning.

3. *Reflection*

Reflection starts with research: observation and analysis of what is actually happening. But then further steps need to be taken, as teachers ask themselves important questions in the light of what they perceive to be actually taking place in their classrooms and schools. These are questions that interrogate what is normally taken for granted, questions such as: Is this what I really want to happen? Why? Is this the best way of ensuring that it does happen? How do I know? The answers to questions such as these can either act as catalysts for change or as confirmation of existing practice.

4. *Reading*

It was clear from talking with Sue that she had read widely during her period of reflection on the writing process. She told me that she was particularly influenced by Nigel Hall's book, *The Emergence of Literacy* (1987). It is part of the professional responsibilities of teachers to ensure that the decisions made are informed decisions, informed by their own experiences and observations but also by the observations and experiences of others. Sue said that she found her reading served to confirm her own feelings and findings and to point her in other directions. It is good to read a wide range of literature – that which supports our own ideas but also that which contradicts us and throws a pebble into the still waters, forcing us to consider other viewpoints.

There are many different influences on the process of change. For some change comes with a bang; for others it emerges with a whimper. Yet for all teachers it is the interrogation of practice that remains central to the on-going development of classroom literacy learning.

The present

I started the emergent approach to writing by changing my classroom into a positive literate environment. An old trolley was found, cleaned and turned into a writing trolley. It contained a variety of writing materials and other aids like sellotape, paper punch and a Petite junior typewriter. The children are encouraged to use this trolley during their free choice activities and two years later it is still a favourite activity area. The writing trolley has since been placed in a developed writing area where there is easy access to tables, reference books, dictionaries, key word charts, children's own notice board, chalk board, etc.

Notices and children's work displayed around the room raise the questions: Can the children read these messages? Are they proud and do they understand their work pinned to the wall?

Relevant books are accessible to the children. Children are encouraged to read, share and make sense.

The home corner constantly needs a variety of print type materials – pencil pads, diaries, menus, children's own telephone directories, birthday cards, books, catalogues, etc.

Children are encouraged to write for a purpose. They are expected to write at least two stories during the week and these are shared individually with a small group, their own class or sometimes another class. Letter writing and cards for all occasions are also encouraged.

Hopefully nothing is taken for granted. All print is shared in a positive and meaningful way.

Let us pause for a moment to consider what Sue has said thus far about her classroom practice. Note how important the context of the literacy learning is; both the physical context, in terms of materials and resources, and the social context of the messages about literacy that are conveyed to the children. These areas will be discussed in greater depth in the following chapter but first it is worth asking ourselves the question, 'Does a change in context automatically mean an increase in motivation, a change in approach and a change in literacy behaviours?'

I am reminded of a child called Christopher whom I once taught. Christopher, at the age of six, was making good progress through the reading scheme but his reading could only be described as stilted, monotone and joyless. The school then abandoned the exclusive use of one scheme and introduced a variety of different fiction and non-fiction books. It was as though Christopher's reading suddenly caught fire – it became animated and Christopher began to enjoy reading and choosing his next book. For Christopher it was certainly true that a change of reading resources dramatically affected his behaviour as a reader. Sue found the same effect in her classroom:

Once the children were motivated it was noticeable that their attitude changed dramatically. They no longer saw writing as a chore. Each child, at whatever level, is encouraged to write and convey meaning, which can be readily accepted and acknowledged by the adult within the room.

During the Autumn Term I was given the post of language co-ordinator for the school and was asked to write the language curriculum. I felt I could only write it along the way of my recent discovery which was the emergent approach. I would have preferred to have had far more staff meetings to discuss and agree on a format but this was not possible. We were a closely-knit staff and my instinct told me that they would support this emergent approach. Fortunately, a colleague from the nursery was willing to help with this demanding task and a year later the language document for the school was completed.

During the summer holiday I felt inspired to write a booklet to help parents understand how we teach writing. A common comment made by parents was an increased awareness of writing activity by their children at home. I sensed that some did not understand what we were trying to do.

Things were going well in the classroom and the nursery classes were doing their best to promote writing with the three- to four-year-olds. I had passed on one set of children who had total experience of the emergent approach, so now the system was working for the three- to six-year-olds in the school.

The icing on the cake came in November 1988 with the published report of the working party that had been set up to formulate the English National Curriculum. It was actually promoting the emergent approach to writing. I was overjoyed!

Four influences on the implementation of change can be identified in Sue's account and we shall consider each of them in turn.

1. *Classroom context*

This issue is discussed fully in the next chapter; it is an important issue and worthy of much thought. Sue began by looking at and changing the resources and organisation of her classroom. Hall (1987) provides a useful checklist for a literacy environment. In it he asks teachers to look at the different physical parts of a classroom and evaluate the extent to which the potential for literacy activity is exploited.

2. *Children's attitudes and behaviour*

One of the most appealing justifications ever used for any approach to teaching is that the children enjoy it. Yet this is the reason of which we must be most wary. Primary children are on the whole very eager to please their teacher and so will seek to do that which gives the reward of praise and a smile. We may never know whether the children really enjoy it, whatever 'it' may be, or whether they enjoy being praised for it, by the teacher who asked them to do it. It is more informative to examine the actual literacy behaviours of the children and to ask if they are behaving as effective and enthusiastic writers and readers. Do they feel confident in handling print? Do they feel able to use print to serve their own purposes? Do they choose to read or write as free activities? Are literacy-based activities an integral part of their play?

These are the sorts of questions that Sue asked herself as she thought about her own approach to literacy learning in her classroom and school. Other teachers, in other times and places, will have other questions which they wish to ask, relating to their own aims. However, the programmes of study of the National Curriculum remain the guideline for planning and analysis of children's behaviour.

3. *Communication*

Whenever change takes place, communication is vital. Human beings, and perhaps teachers more than others, tend to be conservative by nature and to view change with suspicion. If something has appeared to work satisfactorily for several years, why should there be change? Parents' understanding of how children learn to read may be based on their own very different experiences of primary school. Sue found there was a need to explain the new classroom approach because it was affecting what children were doing at home and the parents were asking questions. Often the children themselves are our best advocates!

It is important that other teachers and parents are given clear and valid reasons for what is happening during the implementation of change. Teachers have not been encouraged in the past to communicate to the wider world what they do within their classrooms. In these days of increased accountability, the whole profession must begin to feel less threatened by requests for explanations of what is going on.

4. *Curriculum documents*

As language co-ordinator for the school, Sue was given the task of writing the school's language curriculum document. This was before the introduction of the National Curriculum and so Sue had more freedom than teachers have today. However, she felt that she was only able to write it according to her own beliefs about the nature of literacy learning. She held discussions to inform the rest of the staff about what she was doing. This raises many questions about the function of a school's curriculum document. Does it reflect current practice or that to which one aspires? Is it an agent of change or does it help to maintain the status quo? Is it an expression of reflective critical thinking, or a prescription for 'good practice'?

The National Curriculum was officially introduced by the 1988 Education Reform Act, but schools still have to work out a policy of implementation for themselves. Does this mean that all members of staff will have to work in the same way? Every school will need to consider a number of questions as a whole staff group, just as Sue asked herself personal questions.

Sue's process of change began with dissatisfaction with classroom practice, and moved into a consideration of theory. Other teachers begin with theory and translate that into practice. Whichever route is taken the process of change is a long one and it is hard to define a moment at which it can be said to be finished.

Sue ends her account by looking ahead.

The future

Looking towards the future is difficult but planning ahead is a necessary part of any teaching programme.

My position at school has given me a place of prominence and I am aware that my decisions will possibly have an effect upon others. As the emergent approach to writing is now school policy, new staff should fit in with this policy, particularly as each child will have a language checklist which has to be completed each term by the class teacher.

To take stock of what had already happened at school I devised a questionnaire for staff and called it the 'Emergent Writing Survey'. The answers gathered from this survey were not only interesting but very encouraging.

All the staff except two had been part of the school for four years and so had been aware of my changes and the formation of the school language policy. After the initial apprehension they had all welcomed the emergent approach, particularly as they could see its continuity throughout the school.

One new member of staff, a nursery teacher of wide and varied experience, said that she found this sort of writing taboo years ago in nurseries. However, since adopting this approach there had been a definite change in attitude by the children. Similar comments were made by all the staff on the questionnaire.

Like myself, the staff would welcome visits and talks from others who were using this approach so that difficulties could be discussed and good ideas and practices shared.

The practicalities of organising such visits are major hurdles in themselves. The first step would be to allow teachers occasional visits to a nearby classroom. We all have our strengths and not being able to share these sometimes is such a waste. Having the opportunity to share someone else's expertise was a request made by many colleagues.

Keeping up-to-date with the latest research and recent books/articles, courses, etc. was also suggested as being beneficial.

The questionnaire exercise was useful because it made me aware of staff needs and perhaps these can be given major consideration during future planning.

Gaining support from one's colleagues is one thing but for the system to work successfully one should have support from parents.

Providing parents with the booklet was one of the steps towards helping them to understand how we teach writing.

At school we now have small writing exhibitions on display boards ex-
plaining the different writing stages children pass through. Also, we try to
talk informally each day to parents about their child's progress so that we
don't leave it all to the final open evening.

It is clear from this final part of Sue's account that change is an on-
going process. As teachers we are continually reflecting on practice
and asking how things can be improved. In their answers to Sue's
questionnaire the staff in her school identified three main factors as
being important to them for their further and continuing development:
- visits
- reading
- information

How much are these a 'natural' part of the teaching and learning process? If they are generally considered to be important then
teachers must find time and resources to fit them in. Constant
discussion and reflection by a staff will lead to increased consensus
and so to a consistent and strong approach in a school. There are
always difficulties, though! There was one teacher whose school
had devised a literacy record keeping system based loosely on the
I.L.E.A. *Primary Language Record*. This teacher insisted on adminis-
tering the Schonell reading test to all the children in her class. What
effect does such a difference in philosophy and approach have on
the effectiveness of a school? Should teachers be made to comply –
indeed, *can* they be made to comply?

Throughout this process of discussion and change it could be
argued that a school will create its own literacy. Each school operates
within a particular social context and is its own community. The
literacy within the school will reflect the values and expectations of
both the community of the school itself and the context within which
it is found. Thus a school in a multi-lingual context should reflect that
in the literacy community it creates. The social and political implications of this have been raised in the introduction but there are also
implications in the context of the National Curriculum. It could be
argued that this is regularising the teaching and learning which goes
on in schools and it certainly seems that this was one of the reasons
for setting up the National Curriculum. However, it can be argued
that in forcing schools to discuss and analyse their approaches,
processes of change are set in place that could lead to a variety of
interpretations and developments.

Conclusion

The underlying assumption of this chapter has been the centrality of literacy learning in the primary classroom. It cannot easily be differentiated from other areas of the curriculum and permeates the whole classroom experience.

Different approaches were outlined, ranging from the skills-based approach to that which concentrated on meaning and the existing competencies of children. It was noted that these approaches also differed in their view of learning as either an individual or a social activity. The importance of the classroom context for literacy learning was stressed.

Into this discussion of approaches to literacy was introduced the debate on standards and the evidence that most teachers use a variety of approaches. This multiplicity of approach emphasises the need for teachers to be able to observe and analyse the literacy behaviours of the children in their class and modify their approaches in the light of their new understanding.

The remainder of the chapter chronicled the process of change in one teacher and identified the factors influencing that process. These emerged as:

1 An understanding of the process of literacy learning obtained through observation of children and reading.

2 Discussion with colleagues and a sharing of expertise in order to develop a consistent approach within the school.

3 Statutory requirements on provision and assessment.

The following chapter takes up the issue of the context of literacy learning and explores what messages are conveyed in classrooms about literacy learning.

CHAPTER TWO

Unspoken Messages

Introduction

The unspoken messages of the heading of this chapter refer to the contexts of children's literacy learning. Literacy is not an isolated value-free body of knowledge. It exists within communities and is learned socially by the members of those communities. We also know that what counts as literacy will vary from community to community.

In this chapter I will consider classrooms as communities and look at the literacy experiences of teachers and children in two particular classrooms. There has been much debate in recent months about what is taught in classrooms; the focus of this chapter is what is learned. It is my contention that the two are not necessarily the same; the unspoken messages of the contexts of learning communicate values and ideals which may not be explicit and may not even be conscious. Before going into detailed descriptions of these classrooms I look at our current understandings of the influence of context on children's learning.

The work of Brice Heath (1983) well illustrates the influence of context on children's perceptions and understandings of literacy. The children of Trackton, a black, working-class community, grew up seeing print as an integral part of day-to-day life. Reading was a social activity where the meaning of print was discussed and negotiated by the group and almost always resulted in some form of action. According to Heath, children in Trackton 'read to learn before they go to school to learn to read' (p.191).

In the white, working-class community of Roadville, Heath observes that reading was 'a frequently praised ideal'. Reading was seen as something to be highly valued and parents consciously encouraged their children by surrounding them with all sorts of learning materials, in order that their children might learn to 'do it right'. As Heath says 'Roadville parents believe it their task to praise and practice reading with their young children' (p.234).

It is clear that children learn the literate practices and assumptions which exist within their own community. Heath says that neither the children of Trackton nor the children of Roadville were prepared for the literacy practices of school, because that which they had learned in their home community was very different from that in school and was not recognised or valued. The school itself is a community and as such has its own assumptions and values about literacy learning.

If one accepts that classrooms are social communities, it follows that each community or classroom will have its own definition of literacy. In other words, what counts as valid will vary from classroom to classroom. This will also mean that some literacy behaviours by children will not be recognised or accepted within a classroom. I have told elsewhere the story of Donna which illustrates this point (Jackson 1987).

Donna was in her second term in school. The large first school was a modern semi-open-plan building on a new estate built to cater for overspill from the inner area of a large industrial city. There were more than 400 pupils aged five to eight in the school. Donna's class teacher was also the language consultant for the school.

The teacher told Donna's class to get out writing books, pencils and namecards, and practise writing their names. Donna took a long while to settle. She did not start writing but began examining her namecard closely. She counted the letters, pointed out those which were the same, got up and found both names on the drawers and named each letter. After five minutes the teacher came and told Donna off for not getting on with her work.

Donna had shown herself to be a competent and purposeful beginning literacy learner; her 'failure' at the specified activity was not due to her own inability but because she did not conform to the rather narrow expectations of the teacher. In this short time Donna showed a great deal of knowledge about written language. However, the literacy of the classroom neither accepted nor valued Donna's literate behaviours.

Smith (1983) also viewed literacy as a socio-cultural phenomenon and said that 'Each school develops its own culture (or subculture) of literacy' (p.174). It could also be argued, as we have done here, that each class develops its own culture of literacy.

For if one is to say, as Smith does, that reading and writing are adaptive processes, then within a social context, individual members of a social group bring their own perspectives, engage in their own processes of construction and negotiation and adopt their own literacy behaviours. The nature of literacy within a classroom could be a result of all these individual literacies and be created through processes of negotiation and adaptation. The teacher, who is the most powerful person in the room, will have the greatest influence on the nature of classroom literacy. An individual child's definition of literacy is low in the hierarchy of acceptance and value and often valid literacy events are not recognised, as in the case study of Donna.

In making sense of the community of school, children are continually active in the process of adapting, redefining and recreating their notions of the process of literacy. As Scollon and Scollon (1979) found, educational discussion and practice has concentrated on the essayist forms of literacy to the neglect of those literacies with which young children are frequently competent, such as television, oral story-telling or the functional print of the environment.

The rest of this chapter will consider two classrooms – a mixed reception and Year 1 class and a Year 6 class – as contexts for literacy learning. The teacher will describe how literacy is taught in each class and the resources that are used. Children in the class will then say how they see the literacy learning and resources of their classroom. The analysis of these accounts will focus on environment, resources and practices and will consider the similarities and differences between the classrooms. I will ask the questions:

What is being taught?

What is being learned?

It may well be that the answers to these two questions will not be the same.

The reception class

I consider first Beth's class of 29 reception and Year 1 pupils. The class is a parallel class in a large primary school in an industrial conurbation. Most of the housing surrounding the school is council-owned and a quick tour of the area reveals evidence of much poverty and neglect. The area is a long-established, working-class area and many generations of families have attended the school. Many are supportive of the school and use the staff as their own support system; others see school as an irrelevance and have to be 'encouraged' to send their children to school. The school is typical of fifties design, built in grey concrete with classrooms leading off long corridors.

Beth trained in the early seventies, and has been teaching at this school for the last six years. She has responsibility for art throughout the school and her interest and expertise in the area are evident in the classroom. Displays are large and colourful and refer to work throughout the whole curriculum, inviting the involvement of the children. One corner was devoted to the colour yellow, including the children's own versions of Van Gogh's painting 'The Sunflowers'.

I talked with Beth about the resources for literacy in her classroom and the way in which she structures the teaching of literacy. We began by focussing on reading.

The school uses the *Oxford Reading Tree* scheme and in this classroom are materials from Stage 1 through to 4. There are books, workbooks, flashcards and storytapes. Beth says,

I like this scheme because it's a mixture of stories and words. These children haven't had the experience at home and wouldn't progress if you put them straight on to books.

The *Letterland Scheme* (Wendon 1986) is used for the teaching of phonics and there are also boxes of books which the children are allowed to choose freely to take home. These are known as the library books.

There is no quiet area for books and reading in the classroom. The reading scheme books are stored by stage, housed on shelves in plastic boxes, each clearly labelled with the number of the stage. The library books are in boxes on another surface. Books are an integral part of most of the displays in the classroom and story-telling is an essential and vital part of the day-to-day life of the class. Beth reads a story at least once a day, sometimes from a picture book and sometimes breaking a longer story into instalments. She also tells the children stories and makes up her own stories to tell them, either about the topic under discussion or about the children themselves.

New entrants to the class read the *Reading Tree* big books together as a group and are given the flashcards from Stage 2 to learn. The children work through the books in sequence, learning the words and then reading the books. Each child reads individually to the teacher twice a week and practices his/her flash-cards daily. I observed a daily class reading time. The class was divided into four groups; two worked alone, one with the teacher and one with a parent helper. One of the independent groups played a word-matching bingo game, the other listened to a story tape of one of the scheme books following the text in their own books. The groups with the adults practised word identification. Beth told me that she unashamedly uses 'bribery and corruption to get the children to learn the words'.

The children take their reading books home to practise and also the words, each word written on a small card and placed in a tin, although Beth feels that many of them do not actually do anything with them at home. Each term Beth has a meeting for the parents of new entrants 'to explain how it works and that it's really a mixture of memory and learning the words'.

Let's pause to consider what has already been said before we go on to look at Beth's description of the teaching of writing in her classroom and the children's perspectives on the whole thing.

First we consider the environment. It struck me that there was a great contrast between the kind of literacy evidenced by both the display around the classroom and the use of story in the classroom, and the view of literacy suggested by the formal approach to the teaching of reading. In the classroom displays print was an integral part of the environment, and contained messages and questions in an entertaining, exciting way. On one occasion that I visited the school, Beth told me how before the children had arrived in school that morning she had added text to a picture they had made the previous day. This was in the form of speech bubbles coming out of the figures' mouths; Beth was waiting for the children to notice! When they did she stopped the whole class and they spent a few minutes reading it together and talking about what else the characters might have said. Here was reading as an exciting and integrated part of the curriculum with the children involved in creating and reading texts.

In contrast, the 'reading scheme' remained very much in the hands of the teacher. The children were given flashcards at her discretion from the private depths of her own cupboard and were then told which book from the plastic boxes they were allowed to read next.

The message that this conveyed to me was that reading was something to learn in order to be able to gain access to a world of fun, excitement and adventure; reading in these early stages is a means to an end. Perhaps this was why there was no established book corner as such – the children were not seen as being yet ready to read books for themselves. The display and stories of the classroom were enticing tasters of what was to come once the skill of reading had been mastered. 'Reading is a difficult skill and requires much hard work but is worth it in the end.' This is the unspoken message that the classroom environment conveyed to me; to the children the message might have been completely different.

Second, we look at the resources used. There was a clear distinction made between the reading scheme books and the library books, in location, in availability and in content. The former were highly structured and controlled, the latter were freely available. It will be interesting later to see how the children perceived these differences, for they did indeed notice that the two types of book were not the same.

The use of story in the classroom was interesting. The work of Wells (1987) emphasises the importance of story to children's learning. It is through the construction of stories together that children, through negotiation and collaboration, come to a shared understanding of what an experience means in their particular social context. Through the telling of stories children come to learn the values and expectations of their culture and to make them their own. By experiencing symbolic and reflective language children learn to organise and shape their thoughts and feelings and thus make sense of experiences. Wells says,

> In listening to stories read aloud they not only extend the range of experience they are able to understand but also begin to assimilate the more powerful and more abstract mode of representing experience that is made available by written language. Then, having already discovered one of the chief functions of written language – that of conveying stories – they are prepared for the task of mastering this new medium and the conventions and skills that this involves. (p.200)

I think that this is what was happening in Beth's classroom. The power and efficacy of the storying that was taking place counterbalanced the formal structure of the reading resources and made the classroom an exciting place to be.

Finally, we consider the teaching methods and in so doing look at three statements made by Beth. The first needs little comment at this stage for I have already discussed the value of story in a classroom. Beth expressed her liking for the scheme because 'it's a mixture of stories and words'. This statement reflects, I think, the dilemma which most teachers of young children feel. They want the structure of the 'words' and yet recognise the vital importance of the 'stories'.

In describing her meetings with parents, Beth says they are 'to explain how it works and that it's really a mixture of memory and learning the words'. Nobody is really certain what is involved in the process of learning to read; we know of some things which seem to help and work such as Margaret Clark's *Young Fluent Readers* (1976) has done much to point the way, but we are still very uncertain of what it is that actually happens during the process of becoming a reader. The distinction which Beth makes between memory and learning is an interesting one. Is the difference perhaps a qualitative one in the experience that leads to the final 'knowing', or is it just a semantic difference in terms used for the same process?

Finally, Beth said that the children in her class 'haven't had the experience at home'. This raises the issue of the difference between learning and schooling. Wray, Bloom and Hall (1989) identify the fact that much of the literate activity in schools does not reflect the functional nature of print in the environment. It is the latter with which the majority of children are most familiar and, as illustrated by the work of Heath (1983) schools neither acknowledge nor value home literacies. Because most of us have come from book-orientated homes and work within a book-orientated environment, we assume this is what is required and that anything else is somehow deficient. Consider, however, how many other experiences of print are available to children apart from books: shopping, newspapers and magazines, television, computer games, road signs, clothing, mail, etc. etc. Children have had 'the experience' at home and it is up to us to understand and build on it.

Beth continued to describe the teaching of writing in her classroom.

There is a little table near the teacher's chair on which are pots of pencils and many varieties of crayons and erasers. The children collect what they need at the appropriate time.

The new entrants start by learning letter formation, using the *Letterland* scheme and beginning with the rounded letter shapes e.g. a, d, o, etc. Beth explained to me, 'There's no point in them writing their own news until they can form some letters'. Alongside this, the children also learn to write their own first names, practising daily.

There is a well-determined structure to the development of writing in Beth's class. First the children dictate what they want to say and then either trace or undercopy. When they are copying the shapes reasonably they are given a sentence book. This is a small book in which their dictated writing is written; they copy from here into their own 'writing book'. The next stage comes when they are spacing individual words and hearing and recognising initial sounds – they are then given personal dictionaries. It is at this stage, says Beth, that some of them try out their own spelling.

No unaided writing is done in the classroom. 'They could do it by choice but don't – probably because it's not part of their usual classroom practice.'

We can examine this again using the headings of environments, resources and methods.

There is no clear area for writing in the classroom; activities are set out on each table for the children. The utensils for writing are freely available but there is no paper for 'play writing'. The children have their own books in their drawers but each book has a specific purpose and is used for teacher-directed activities. It seems to me that a key issue for understanding literacy in this classroom is the issue of 'ownership'. To whom does the classroom as an environment for writing belong? Both the environment and the resources indicate that writing in this classroom belongs to the teacher. She controls the books, is very near to the utensils and determines what sort of writing is done when.

The practices of this classroom regarding writing link together transcription and authorship and it is this connection which I wish to discuss further. Hall (1989) defines authorship as 'the reflective generation of written text' and distinguishes it quite clearly from the skills of transcription. Hall does not de-value the skills of spelling, punctuation and neat handwriting but rather considers them as,

> ... contributions to the more effective realisation of authorship ... as contributions they take their place alongside the development of other authorial abilities and do not dominate or displace them. (p.xiv)

Hall would argue that, despite a lack of transcriptional skills, children are able to behave as authors. It is this belief which underpinned Sue's emerging philosophy, described in the previous chapter.

Differences in practice reflect a fundamental difference in models of learning. A skills-based model of learning is founded on a defecit view of children's understanding. This is accompanied by a view of teaching as a form of instruction, as a transmission of skills and knowledge. The teacher possesses the knowledge and skills and passes them on to the pupils, who are seen as lacking in them. Thus the whole question of the nature of literacy can be seen as being unproblematic. Literacy is perceived in terms of a clear set of understandings and skills which can be broken down into stages for ease of transmission. The relationship between teaching and learning within this model is also seen as being relatively unproblematic; what is taught is learned and what is not taught is not learned.

However, if teachers recognise and value the children's existing understandings and knowledge and see them as playing an important part in the children's learning, the nature of how literacy competence occurs changes. If children have already learned a lot about print and how it works from previous experiences, teaching becomes a matter of helping them to apply that knowledge to new situations and to refine their strategies for dealing with print. Learning can no longer be seen as a hierarchical linear development but rather as a cyclical process. A teacher who recognises this and holds a positive view of children as active literacy learners is likely to enter into a process of negotiation with the children about the nature of the literacy experiences in their classroom and to give the children space to recreate their own classroom literacy.

Butler and Turbill (1984) describe the implications for classroom practice of adopting a view of literacy learning as a process. First, time for practice and listening is essential. Children need time both to behave as readers and writers and to see and hear experienced readers and writers in action. Second, the issue of ownership is crucial; children need to be given control and responsibility for their own literate activites. Then there will be opportunities for process (drafting, editing and re-reading) and for conference (sharing with and benefiting from the expertise of experienced readers and writers). Finally, there will be all the resources available to enable the children to read and write.

Having looked at and examined the teacher's understanding of her classroom as a context for literacy learning, let us now explore the children's understanding of the same classroom and see if they have picked up and interpreted any of the same unspoken messages.

I talked to Craig, Chantelle and Jennifer. To each of them I said, 'I'm interested in how people learn to read and write. Can you tell me how reading and writing works in your classroom?' Craig was first. I give the children's comments just as they were spoken to me with my own questions and interjections in italics. Craig speaks with a Black Country dialect and I have attempted to reproduce this in my transcription.

My teacher writes on my book so I can copy it in my other book. I've got a big book – it's bigger than my little book. *What about reading?* I cor read. I'm six now. I cor read. Some children in the big class con but I cor. *Do you have a reading book?* Spot. Spot is a library book that goes in that shelf. The reading book goes in that shelf. *How do you decide which book to have?* The library van comes to sell the books. The library chooses them. You don't have to pay and you choose any book you like. I'm on new reading ones. I used to be on green but now I'm on blue. Blue are the oldest ones and green are baby ones; they're just little books. I can read my reading book but not my library book. *Why not?* It's got harder words in it. *How do you know which reading book to have?* Miss M... decides what book, she reads it on the back. *Do you read at home?* I read books from another library and comics. I don't do no writing at home. I do different things to drawing pictures at home. *How do you learn to read?* I cor read so I practised it. I never had words to learn; I had some new words. Miss M... writes them down on a piece of paper and I just read to her. I have to say the names and that's it.

Chantelle was next and began by talking about writing.

Are you a good writer? A bit. I make up stories and numbers. I write news and make up books. Miss M... tells us what to write. I get the letter, show it to Miss M... and then she writes it when you tell her what to write. *Do you write at home?* Capital letters. It's different at home and at school, you're not allowed to do them at school. *What about reading?* Miss M... helps me. She just says the word. If I don't know the word 'and' she would say it. *How do you know what book to read?* Because it's at the back of the book – of the reading ones. *What are the reading ones?* They're in a different box kept separately on the shelf box. I can choose my own book from any box.

What if the book you chose was too difficult? I wouldn't be able to read it and I'd choose another one. Miss M... helps me choose. *How did you learn to read?* Mrs D... always read a book for me and I've forgotten. *Do you read at home?* Yes. I have to read my reading book at home. Mum tells me when to stop cos she needs to stop. Sometimes I read to myself. When I get stuck I tell Dad and he tells me the word. Sometimes I read to myself and sometimes to Mum. I like reading to myself cos I do. I've got different books at home. I haven't got some books but I've got thousands.

Lastly, I spoke to Jennifer.

I'm good at reading, because she's ticked nearly every word. *What book are you reading?* A birdie blue book. I'm past the green and blue books, the reds are after. The red books are going to have three lines. The green books have one or two lines. I can't remember not being able to read. *How did you learn to read?* By sounding out. My mum's learning to sound it. I've got a desk, a typewriter and paper at home. I practise with my writing card. I've learned spelling by my mum. *How does Miss M... help you?* By teaching about dogs and cats and things like that. Also we watch the telly sometimes.

All of these children were very clear about the structure of the programme of literacy learning in their classroom and it is easy for us, from their descriptions, to know at what stage of the system they are.

The children were also very clear about the hierarchical development and used sneering expressions about the stages they had passed. Craig dismissed the blue books as the 'baby ones'. For them the idea of harder meant 'harder words' or 'more lines'. Is this not true of many adult perceptions of levels of difficulty? Yet consider a book such as *Time to get out of the bath, Shirley* by John Burningham – a book with very few simple words and yet requiring sophisticated behaviour as a reader if one is to make full sense of it. There are many books such as this which can be read at different levels, an idea which we shall discuss later in this book.

Consider also the children's idea of what it meant to become a reader and writer. They had clear ideas about 'being taught' and all of them, when asked about how they learned to read, replied in some way about 'being told'. They had been given words to learn, they were told what to write, they were not allowed to use capital letters. Jennifer saw herself as being a reader and her understanding of this came from what the teacher had done, that is ticked all the books on the list. According to Jennifer she had read all the books and so must be a good reader.

There was a clear distinction in the children's minds between literacy at home and literacy in school. The main distinction seems to be that at home they had choice and variety in what they could do, whereas what was allowed at school was tightly determined. The exception seems to be Jennifer, who believes that she does most of her 'real' learning at home. One wonders what a lay inspector would make of such a comment!

The 'unspoken messages' which these children had learned about literacy were that it is a highly structured thing which they are being taught. Implicit in their comments seems to be the idea that literacy in school is something which is passed on to them by an adult, usually the teacher. In Jennifer's case this message was reinforced at home, where her parents seemed also to be acting as the experts with skills to pass on. The children were very aware of what they could not do and of how they compared with the rest of their peer group.

The theme of 'ownership' seems helpful in understanding perceptions of literacy learning in this class. These young children saw literacy as something which they were to learn by passing through very clear stages which had been devised by the teacher. The teacher herself saw literacy in this way and had clear justifications for the structure of her teaching programme. However, the strong use of story within the classroom and the exciting use of the oral tradition gave back some of the ownership to the children and gave them the opportunity to use some of their experiences from home at school. In this use of symbolic and reflective language they were given a way into the more formal learning of literacy.

We have so far considered the literacy learning of young children at the beginning of their school career. Let us now go to the other end of the primary school and look at two Year 6 classrooms.

There are two parallel Year 6 classes in this large primary school situated in a suburban area. The catchment area of the school is predominantly privately-owned houses, interspersed with some council-owned property. Many of the families living here are blue collar workers or young couples at the start of their career. The two classes are in adjacent classrooms and are both very similar in appearance and content. The tables are arranged in groups and most of the time the children work independently. Display is done by the children. There are piles of books and papers around the rooms, which have the atmosphere of workshops in action. I spoke to both teachers and to children from both classes. I start with the teachers' description of how literacy learning is organised within their classes. Jackie was first.

By the time they get to Year 6 the children are all free readers. They are expected to have a book or some form of reading material, either fiction or non-fiction and I don't mind where they get it from. They read in spare moments through the day. I don't keep any records of what they read. I encourage them to read for pleasure. I also read to them – novels and poetry. Lower down the school the *Oxford Reading Tree* scheme is used. The very poor ones get special help. It doesn't matter what they read as long as it's something; they read a variety of forms through the year.

I then spoke to Maggie.

The children get their books out at 9.00 a.m. and read for half an hour every day. The reading scheme in the junior part of the school is *Oxford Junior Readers* and *Wide Range Readers* with fiction slotted in. Most of the children in my class are free readers and choose from the school library or bring books from home. I keep several types of record. There are school-produced sheets which show a child's reading age at the end of each year. We do the Burt test. I keep a list of what each child reads and when each child reads to me. I try to hear each child every three weeks and at least once a month. The poorer ones I hear much more often. They also get special help from the support teacher.

A lot of non-fiction is read in topic work. Sometimes they all do the same topic but usually they do group or individual topics. I don't teach any information skills as that has usually been done before.

Most of the writing the children do is factual, linked with their topic work. They do not do so much creative work in this year. They draft each piece of work. Sometimes we do comprehensions.

We have a spelling lesson every week and a spelling test each week as well.

It is interesting to compare what these teachers told me with what Southgate et al found in their study *Extending Beginning Reading* (1981). There are many similarities: teachers reading a variety of materials aloud to their pupils, little direct teaching in what Southgate calls 'bibliographical skills', minimal time devoted to hearing individual children read.

Returning to our theme of 'ownership' it would appear that

these older children are much more in control of their own learning. In terms of resources, the environment and the practice, the children are frequently very much left to their own devices. The teacher's role is that of a facilitator and helper, guiding and responding to the children. What are the implications of this? What are the unspoken messages conveyed in these classrooms?

There is very much a sense that these children have already learned to read and write and that in this classroom the concern is to get on and 'do it'. Both the teachers used the familiar phrase 'free reader' to mean that the children had worked their way through the scheme, could now read and so it was up to them what they read. The fact that the children could read seemed to be more important than what they read and how they read it. Those who were having difficulties with reading went outside the classroom for special help, the implication being that 'in this room we can all read. The teaching of reading does not take place here'.

Literacy was seen very much as a tool for other things, topic work, for example, and much of the children's writing and reading was of non-fiction. There was little talk of responding to and creating different forms of texts. It is true that the children were all reading a variety of genres and yet there was little talk about their reading or their response to the texts. The literacy demands which were made of the children in other areas of the curriculum, and during the course of their topic work were extensive and yet neither teacher mentioned how the children were helped with this. This does not necessarily mean of course that it was not done but that these teachers did not see it as relevant when they were talking about literacy in their classrooms.

The 'unspoken message' of this classroom seemed to me to be 'Now we can all read and write and know what to do, let's get on with it and use what we know to find out other things.' Despite a strongly held belief in the importance of reading for pleasure it seemed that much of the literacy work in the classrooms was of a functional nature and used a narrow range of formats. Reading for pleasure was seen as a time filler when work was finished or registration being done and so could appear to be marginalised.

How did the children see this? I talked to several children from both classes. Again I repeat their comments exactly as they were made to me with my interjections in italics. Mark was first.

Can you tell me about reading and writing in your class? We read a lot in topic work – we have a lot of sheets – and we read books when we have no work to do. I choose what book to read by reading the back of books. I like fantasy books. The books in school are all out of date, for example they have 'The Pied Piper' which no-one would be seen dead reading. I get books from the school library and the public library. I read when I've finished my work. The reading scheme we had was utterly boring and repetitive and didn't hold any interest. They were called the ...... Readers. I skipped some of the books. *Can you remember learning to read?* When I was three my mum decided to read to me and I said the words after her. I read books like Postman Pat. *What about writing?* We have times to write about things. I like creating characters. I do a draft in my rough book, I flick through books for ideas and then I make changes. We also do comprehension, note passing and diaries. I don't do much reading these days but when I do my mind slips into the book and my body gets left in the classroom.

Jane told me,

I prefer Maths writing because you can get the setting out right. I can't do English writing so well because you don't know how it's supposed to be.

I talked to Katie and Rebecca together and so their comments have been put together.

Reading is hard. You have to read in silence. Sometimes if you read aloud it's easier to understand. If you make a mistake when you're reading to the teacher you get corrected and everybody thinks you're a fool. It's bad to get things wrong. We don't read to the teacher very often. I don't like it because I can make a muck-up. It's embarrassing because there are boys by Miss B's table. We're free readers. We've passed all the easier books. I don't like books of short stories, they cut out the interesting bits. I prefer long books. We have silent reading every morning for half an hour. I don't like it. It's too long and stops me talking. It's better because if I don't know a word I can skip it but then it stops me understanding. If there are six hard words I skip on a page I read it three times over to understand. Topic is good. We have sheets but sometimes we have to read paragraphs out and that's embarrassing. *Can you remember how you learned to read?* The teacher learned us. She went through words with us and learned us how to say them. We had cards in margarine tubs to take home to learn like 'as' and 'and'. My mum read them to me and I said them. We had purple cards with our name on to read every day. We were learning more complicated words. My mum wrote stories for me to read. The teacher used to write and leave a space for me to copy. She decided what to write. *What about writing now?* We've been doing joined up writing since Year 4. We write stories. We don't write news any more – you know like what you did at the weekend and in the holiday – and I love doing that. I write stories at home. At school we write about facts in topic. We write notes when someone is speaking. You get a sticker if you put in good words or sentences or if it's neat or if there are good illustrations.

I will consider what the children thought about reading in school first. There were strong individual differences between the children at this age. It is easy to assume an 'average' because all the children are able to read and yet they are all different in their behaviour as readers. Mark, who spoke to me first, was a very bright and articulate boy and a fanatical reader of one series of fantasy novels. He knows something really important about read- ing, as illustrated by his phrase, 'my mind slips into the book'. It would be interesting to introduce him to other examples of this genre and try to broaden his reading diet and sharpen his critical faculties. All the children were very aware of their likes and dislikes in reading and seemed ready for more detailed work on critical analysis of texts. Notice how important understanding a text was to two of them. They didn't like reading silently because they found it harder to understand that way and they were prepared to reread a page several times until they understood it.

The sense of progression was as clear in this class as it was at the lower end of the other primary school. These 11-year-olds remem- bered how it was to learn to read, were aware of their own progress through the stages and of their present status as 'free readers'.

In analysing the literacy learning in Beth's classroom I used the notion of 'ownership' to explore the idea of a classroom literacy. Our discussion accepted the assumption that most valid literacy activity comes through teacher-initiated and directed activities and that control is in the hands of the teacher who has the choice whether or not to hand over part or all of the ownership of the learning to the children. This assumption lies open to question, for it surely must be that children modify and adapt even those events which are firmly owned by the teacher.

The control of the teacher and the 'official, accepted' literacy was clear within the two Year 6 classes. Jane did not like English writing in school because she did not know what was right and wrong. After six years in school she had received the message that there is a clear right and wrong and took every opportunity to avoid the chance of being found wrong. Katie and Rebecca said 'It's bad to get things wrong.' Here we see schooling and literacy closely linked in the minds of the children and perhaps the schooling aspect getting in the way of literacy learning.

This distinction was also clear in the children's views of the resources for reading available at home and school. Mark was vociferous in his dislike for the scheme but also for the books which were available in school. One 'would not be seen dead' reading them and they were totally 'out of date'. Mark thus viewed his own reading material as not validated by the school. He saw learning to read as a matter of getting through the scheme as quickly as possible in order to be able to take control of his own reading and reject that which was offered by the school.

The public nature of reading is something which several children, in particular Kate and Rebecca, commented on. The practice of the classroom required times when reading was a performance; none of the children enjoyed this aspect at all and took all means possible to avoid it. They were aware that judgements were being made of them as readers on their performance and did not think this a fair assessment of their competencies.

I have discussed in this chapter the fact that all is not immediately apparent when it comes to exploring literacy learning in primary classrooms. There are many unspoken messages which the children pick up and interpret according to their own understandings and the contexts in which they operate. We have seen how the concept of ownership can be helpful in our attempts to find out what is going on and what are the prevalent values. One thing which is clear is that the relationship between teaching and learning is not a simple one.

In the next chapter I go on to look at how children become readers and to explore the connections between children's actual reading behaviour and the requirements and assessment practices of the National Curriculum.

CHAPTER THREE

How do Children Become Readers?

Introduction

I said in the previous chapter that we really know very little about how children learn to read. In this chapter I hope to try to explore that issue a little further. By looking at transcripts of children interacting with books I shall attempt to see what happens as meaning is created.

In the study of literacy learning, emphasis has recently been placed on the experiences young children bring to school with them (Harste, Woodward and Burke 1984). The use of the term 'emergent literacy' implies that literacy is something that emerges from existing knowledge and understanding. Let us pause for a moment and consider what this means in more detail.

Young children growing up in our society are exposed to a vast amount of print in various forms, being used in various ways. Print comes into the home in many different ways: on packets, junk mail, newspapers and magazines, letters, circulars, the television and computer screens, calendars, pictures, scribbled notes, bills, and so on. Many young children and adults wear print emblazoned across the front of their T-shirts and track suits. Outside there is just as much print: road signs, posters, shop signs, bus notices, house names, car number plates etc. All this print is an integral part of the day-to-day life of members of the community. It tells them where to go, what to buy, which bus to catch, what day it is, the latest news, how much milk is required on that day. Children live in this print saturated world and they see print being used by adults and older children who are competent print users.

I think of one typical day in my life. I get up and check the time on the clock. I shower and dress, reading the labels on the shampoo and conditioner bottles to make sure I use them in the correct order. I go and get my baby daughter up and dressed and then take her downstairs to get breakfast. In order to do this I need to make sure that each person has the required breakfast cereal, which involves reading three different packets! Over breakfast, my husband and I check the wall calendar and diaries for our plans for the day. Once at work I prepare for teaching sessions, read and mark essays and draft course outlines for the following term. On the way home I call in at the shop for a few things on my shopping list that I was unable to get at the weekend. During the evening at home I watch the television, glance over the newspaper and sort out some correspondence, writing cheques to pay bills and filling in forms. Finally, in bed, I read several chapters of a novel before going to sleep.

That example gives just a few incidents of literacy behaviour in which I engage during the course of a 'normal' day. I have used print to inform, to remind, to persuade, to keep in touch, to amuse, to instruct and to disturb. There are many more purposes of print that we could each describe. It would be impossible to imagine life without print.

Young children are surrounded with print and with people using print. There is evidence that most young children are given opportunities to behave as readers, writers and mark makers. They have crayons, colouring books and pencils; they have books and comics; many of them have access to a computer keyboard and screen. On the whole it would appear that adults respond to the child's use of print in a way which ascribes meaning to it, just as they respond to the baby's first babblings as meaningful speech.

Ferreiro and Teberosky (1983) and Harste, Woodward and Burke (1984), although approaching the study of early literacy from differing perspectives, all agree that young children learn to deal with print by 'having a go'. As Wray, Bloom and Hall (1989) say, 'Early childhood is a continual process of experimentation, risk-taking and negotiation, in purposeful, intentional ways' (p.61).

We shall consider the psychological perspective of Ferreiro and Teberosky more closely in the next chapter when we consider the beginnings of writing. Harste, Woodward and Burke see literacy as a process and believe that children come to understand it in a social sense. They use what they already know in bringing strategies to a problem in order to make sense of it. Harste et al identify four main strategies: negotiation, risk-taking, intentionality and fine tuning. It is the ability to draw on a variety of strategies that enables a child to be the most effective literacy learner. Children use what they already know in order to make sense of a new problematic situation.

The approaches to early reading that stress 'meaning' (Goodman 1976, Smith 1978) see reading as an essentially sense-making process, in which children bring meanings to and take meanings from a text through an active engagement with it. Literacy learning is seen as a continuation of oral language learning; children make sense of the language they continually see around them, and are involved in an active process of learning, responding as readers and writers and continually refining behaviours in the light of new experiences.

Many teachers, including those who are now using 'real' books to facilitate literacy learning rather than a packaged scheme, are redefining their role as enablers and facilitators rather than as instructors; the emphasis has moved from teaching to learning. Children's stories are seen as conveying their understanding about how the world works and their attempts to bring meaning to their experiences. In the social context of a classroom adults and children together negotiate and share meanings. The teacher engages in this process of integration as a co-learner with the children, for, as Margaret Meek (1988), said,

> ...what they (the children) think and say about what they know and understand is carried by the words they use. As adults we too can make meanings...of what they say and do. But sometimes, when we hear children stretching and enhancing this ability, we may wonder if we make the most of this ability when we engage in the interventions we call teaching. The emphasis shifts to the learners. Intervention is replaced by interaction. (p.2)

I shall go on to consider later in the chapter how this description of teaching and learning fits in with current legislation about what happens in schools and classrooms.

If one looks back over some of the major publications dealing with literacy within the last two decades (for example, Bullock 1975, Galton and Simon 1980, Southgate 1981, Tizard et al 1988, Kingman 1988, not to mention the National Curriculum documentation) it is interesting to note how classroom literacy has been described and to examine the terms that are used to talk about literacy learning. The Bullock Report (1975) placed great emphasis on world recognition and identified the main priority of

early literacy as building up a sight vocabulary. While recognising the importance of enjoyment and thus of understanding in
early reading, the Report's definition of reading was in terms of
skills. These were broken down into primary skills (shape recognition and sound symbol correspondence), intermediate skills (se-
quences of letters and words) and comprehension skills (interactions between the author's meanings and the reader's purpose).
Although not specifically stated, it was implicit in the use of these
terms that reading is a hierarchical skill system; the statement that a
reading scheme will form the core of most reading activity in the
early years supports this assumption.

In 1980 the ORACLE project (Galton and Simon), using systematic observation techniques, considered performance in 58
junior classrooms. The project's description of literacy is, once
again, very much in terms of skills. The researchers used a mul-
tiple-choice test which looked at word identification, comprehension skills, punctuation and spelling. The project *Extending Beginning Reading* (Southgate, Arnold and Johnson 1981) again used
systematic observation and standardised reading tests to study
over 140 first and second year junior children. The report described learning to read as a developmental process and stated that
progress towards effective reading involves ever-expanding mas-
tery of more advanced skills (p.6). Alongside this essentially skill-
based view, the beginnings of a problem-solving approach can be
perceived. The researchers, while focussing on the identification of
skills, also mention competencies, and one of their aims was to
determine the strategies children adopt. It could be that the recognition of literacy learning as a process was starting.

The last two projects discussed have focussed on the junior age
range; do descriptions of early literacy learning concentrate more
on sense making processes? The H.M.I. survey of 80 first schools
in England (D.E.S. 1982) found that teachers gave reading the
highest priority within the curriculum, and that the most successful schools used a combination of teaching methods. However, the
study also criticised an emphasis on decoding print which it was
said led to mechanical reading and little understanding. In a study
at a similar time, Wells (1981) placed an emphasis on story-telling
and listening to stories as central to literacy development. Of all
literacy-related activities of pre-school children, Wells identified
listening to a story as the only one significantly associated with
success in literacy at age seven.

In contrast, Tizard et al (1988), in their study of young children's attainment and progress in school, found that the strongest predictor of reading ability at age seven was the number of letters a child could identify at the age of four and three-quarters. While acknowledging that learning to read is a complex process, which includes 'extracting the meanings of a written passage' (p.169), Tizard claimed that there is a causal relationship between early letter identification and later literacy attainment. This claim is based on two arguments; first that learning to read includes attending to the structure of words and second, that children who possess these skills on entry to school are more likely to be given reading books before children without them.

Woodhead (*Times Educational Supplement* 1988) identified the danger of this sort of analysis, assessing children's attainment merely by skills valued by adult society and not acknowledging the children's own learning priorities. He quoted his daughter saying, 'Don't turn the page yet, Daddy – I haven't finished looking at the pictures,' as an example of adult 'sophistication', neglecting the 'broader possibilities for learning' that children retain.

It would seem appropriate to look now at some young children reading and explore what is actually happening in terms of their understanding of the texts. We shall then go on to relate what we find to current ways of describing and recording reading behaviours. We explore how both they and their teacher tackle the texts.

Cameron was eight years old at the time when he was reading to his teacher, who was recording his reading for her own purposes and let me have a copy of the tape. He had experienced difficulties with his reading and was receiving some help from the special needs teacher which was heavily phonic-based. His teacher reported that he had begun to make 'real progress' during the last two terms. He was reading from H.E. Todd's book *Bobby Brewster's First Fun*. This was a book he had chosen for himself from the class library.

1 **Teacher:** Right Cameron, would you like to start?
2 **Cameron:** One morning Bobby Brewster was lying in bed when he…saw the fly…a fly walking up in up the wall and across the selling.
3 **T:** Now, what's it likely to be? Not selling but…?
4 **C:** Ceiling.
5 **T:** Ceiling. Good boy.

6 **C:** Up upside down without going bonk on its head. Bobby Brewster which…watched

7 **T:** Good boy.

8 **C:** it for a little while and then said to himself, 'I wish that fly would touch me…teach me

9 **T:** Good.

10 **C:** How to walk up the wall and across the ceiling up upside down without going bonk on his head (*teacher laughs*)…at last

11 **T:** at…

12 **C:** at least

13 **T:** Good boy.

14 **C:** he thought he said it to himself but he ca…can't have done because a funny thi…thing happened. The fly answered him it did really. I c…couldn't do that said the fly. Of course Bobby Brewster was very…sure

15 **T:** No. What do you think he felt like when he heard this fly talking to him? What would he have been? What would you have been if a fly suddenly talked to you?

16 **C:** A bit surprised.

17 **T:** Yes. So what do you think this word is?

18 **C:** Surprised.

19 **T:** It is, so carry on.

20 **C:** at …hearing

21 **T:** Good boy.

22 **C:** the fly talk at all when if you are clever enough to speak said Bobby Brewster suddenly

23 **T:** No.

24 **C:** surely

25 **T:** surely

26 **C:** you're you're clever enough to touch

27 **T:** tee…

28 **C:** teach me

29 **T:** Good

30 **C:** how to walk up the wall and across the ceiling upside down without going bonk on my head. (*teacher laughs*) I may…

31 **T:** Mm, mm. That's right.

32 **C:** be clear

33 **T:** Think again.

34 **C:** clever enough said the fly but my friends would never let me you see a it isn't adven…

35 **T:** It isn't…

36 **C:** it isn't advant

37 **T:** Think again.

38 **C:** much fun being a fly but one of the fl…flu…fly…few

39 **T:** Good.

40 **C:** adventurers

41 **T:** Now let's sound it out, shall we — have a try — what does it say?

42 **C:** ad — van — ta — tage

43 **T:** Now — what's that?

44 **C:** advant…

45 **T:** Run them closely together then.

46 **C:** advan…tage

47 **T:** We don't say advantage, we say advantige, don't we?

48 **C:** advantage

49 **T:** One of the few advantages. What's an advantage? What does it mean when you say one of the few advantages about…I might say one of the few advantages — very very few — of being a teacher is having a long holiday. So it means one of the good things, one of the special things. O.K.? So one of the advantages of being a fly is that you can walk up the wall which nobody else can do can they? Right.

50 **C:** If you had those suckers…

51 **T:** Suckers, that's right…is that you can walk up the wall and a…

52 **C:** across the ceiling upside down without going bonk on your head. If I told you how to do it it wouldn't be a fly secret would it. 'No. I suppose not,' said Bobby Brewster, 'but it's a… pint…

53 **T:** Now — think about the letters. Sound the letters. What does it begin…

54 **C:** pity

55 **T:** Pity. Good boy.

56 **C:** all the same. The fly went on walking up the wall and then suddenly it stopped. 'I tell you what,' said the fly, 'I'll make a bargain with you.' 'I don't know what a bargain is,' said Bobby Brewster (*laughs*). 'Well,' said the fly, 'if you will… leave a nice… pheasant

57 **T:** Now – look at the letters. What are those two going to say together?

58 **C:** feast

59 **T:** Yes. Do you remember we talked about that, didn't we… two vowel men go walking, the first one does the talking. Yea?… feast for me

60 **C:** for me and my friends out in the garden tonight. I'll come here again tomorrow morning and touch

61 **T:** and I'll…

62 **C:** i'll touch

63 **T:** tee… tee…

64 C: teach you how to walk up the wall and across the ceiling upside down without going bonk on your head.

This is the sort of interchange going on between teachers and pupils every day, which teachers use to evaluate children's behaviour as readers. A lot of that evaluation is done during a reading session and much is never recorded; yet teachers are continually making judgements about children's understandings and competencies. Let's examine Cameron's reading a little more closely and try to make some of those judgements more overt, remembering that judgements we make here are out of context and without any prior knowledge of Cameron as a reader.

Cameron makes several 'errors' in his reading which he self-corrects; this can be seen as an indication that Cameron is gaining some meaning from the text and is following the sense of the story. However, in line four Cameron is not aware that he has made an error and the teacher stops him to draw attention to this. She points out to him that what he has said does not make sense and encourages him to look at the meaning and to correct his miscue. It would seem that Cameron used phonic strategies in his original attempt to read the word and these by themselves let him down in his attempt to make meaning. He read 's' for the initial sound which set him off on the right track, then he did not know the medial vowel blend but got the last part of the word. It would appear that the teacher recognised how his phonic knowledge had failed him and was showing him that there were other strategies he could use which would be helpful in this context.

In lines six and eight Cameron self-corrects, using meaning as his main strategy. In line ten the teacher underlines this emphasis on meaning by responding to the story as a listener. Her laughter shows Cameron that what he is reading is a story that other people can listen to and enjoy.

In lines 14, 27, and 35 the teacher again corrects Cameron's miscues by encouraging him to use semantic or meaning-based strategies. In line 14 Cameron's reading of 'sure' is a very good attempt at the first half of 'surprised' but his over-reliance on one strategy means that he is not able to use the sense of the story to help him go further in his decoding.

Line 38 is an interesting attempt by Cameron to read the word 'few'. He makes several attempts at the word and again these are phonically based. He starts with 'fl...' and ends with 'few'. It is only when he realises that the first sound is not 'fl' that he is able to read the word correctly. Again it can be argued that the meaning of the sentence must have some contribution to make at this point in order for Cameron to make sense of the text.

In line 40 Cameron is beginning to combine the graphophonic and semantic strategies. The result makes some sort of sense but does not fit in with the language pattern of the sentence. Cameron also needs to make use of the syntactic cue system; he reads 'advant' well but then replaces it with something more meaningful semantically.

For the first time in line 41 the teacher encourages Cameron to use the graphophonic cue system and supports him in word building; Cameron's response in line 42 suggests that this is a strategy with which he is all too familiar. Once he has 'read' the word she then goes on to explain it to him so that he can make sense of the text. This is a good illustration of the inter-reliance of the cue systems and how over-reliance on one is not enough for a complete understanding of a text. Cameron responds to the meaning and is quite willing to be distracted by a discussion on insects but the teacher brings his attention back to the text.

In line 53 the teacher goes straight in to using phonics, asking Cameron to sound out the word. Cameron, however, reads the word correctly without sounding it out aloud. It could be, that Cameron is able to use each strategy effectively but needs help in realising which strategy is most appropriate. Indeed as Frank Smith says, you can only use phonic strategies when you already know what the word is.

In line 56 Cameron himself laughs at an amusing point in the story, showing that he is following the sense of the story and responding to it as a reader. The teacher here picks up on a miscue that Cameron has made and focusses in on the medial vowel blend.

The reading process

I have looked at one child and his behaviour as a reader when engaged with one particular text. I have also discussed to a certain extent the role of the teacher in Cameron's development as a reader. I shall now go on to relate this analysis and discussion to our current understanding of the process of reading and the requirements of an effective reading programme.

Bettelheim and Zelan (1982) say, '...learning to read must give the child the feeling that, through it, new worlds will be opened in his mind and imagination.' How can we, as teachers, enable all children to have that feeling and experience through the context we create and the materials we provide for the learning of reading?

It seems an obvious point and yet one that is often forgotten that in order to be able to read, children must have some idea of what reading is, of the purposes it serves and the forms it takes. In other words, children need to have some awareness of reading as a whole process before they can begin to consider its constituent parts. Concentration on the latter at the expense of a full appreciation of the former can, as Liz Waterland (1985) said, lead to 'children who have been taught to read but have failed to learn it' (p.3). Imagine trying to break down into its constituent parts the process of changing gear in a car. The operation rapidly becomes extremely complex and very difficult to understand! It is far easier to sit in a car and experience the process at first hand: to feel the bite on the clutch, to hear the changing sound of the engine and to learn by having a go, in spite of the distinct likelihood of the gears crashing on several attempts! Learning to read is a similar process: to analyse and dissect makes it seem very complex and unintelligible and yet very many children become fluent readers and gain much pleasure from the world of print. What is it that enables them to do this?

I have already outlined the vast experience of print which the majority of young children have. They see print used in a wide variety of ways; print is an integral part of day-to-day life. Pearson (1987) conducted an experiment with a group of five-year-olds to see how many words from their everyday environment they could recognise. He used words such as *Asda*, *The 'A' Team*, *Ariel*, *The Sun* and *Toyota*. Only a few of the children could recognise the words when presented in handwritten form but when presented in the print style commonly associated with each word, 50% of the children recognised the words. When shown the words in the context in which they were normally seen most of the children could recognise all of the words. Print was a part of the children's normal environment and carried meaning for them, in that environment, not as isolated, disembodied items of handwritten script.

As well as being experienced observers of print, young children are also experienced language users. In a short space of time, the vast majority of young children learn to use language to communicate effectively, and a great deal about how language works. They

understand the usual flow of language and will notice when something does not quite fit. They may not be able to use the conventional terms for different parts of speech but understand different
forms and their functions.

It is with this solid understanding of language and print that
young children begin the process of becoming readers; it is this
understanding that will help them learn, if the reading programme
allows. Let us explore how this works more closely.

A well loved children's book is *Peace at Last* by Jill Murphy. This
begins, 'The hour was late. Mr Bear was tired, Mrs Bear was tired
and Baby Bear was tired, so they all went to...' What is the final
word in that sentence? If a young child did not know, what would
help him/her to work it out? There are three cue systems which
can be used; they can be implemented in any order and their use
is often implicit rather than explicit. For the sake of illustration
here, the process is made much more overt than it would usually
be in practice. First, the child could look at the picture accom-
panying the text. It shows the Bear family, dressed in their night
clothes, going up the stairs. Mrs Bear is yawning widely. So we
have several clues – it is late, and they are going upstairs, dressed
in their sleep clothes. What does our experience of life lead us to
guess that they might be doing? Second, knowledge of language
and how it works helps the child to make more sense of the text.
The child's experience of language leads him/her to reject guesses
such as '...they went to yawning/pyjamas/upstairs.' Each of these
ideas is associated with the content of the sentence but do not fit its
syntax; and so a more informed guess is made. It could say, '...they
went to sleep/wash/bed'. How does the child know which of these
guesses is the right one? Third, s/he looks at the word itself and
uses his/her knowledge of print to help. The child now sees that the
word starts with 'b', and so immediately refines the guess to 'bed'.
Knowledge of life, of books, of language and of the graphophonic
nature of print has helped the child to read this text. With the
support of an experienced reader the young child can make meaning from the text.

It is these types of knowing that form the constituent parts of
reading; when these parts work together we are able to make sense
of and gain meaning from a text.

There are syntactical cues in the text that help the reader to draw
on knowledge of both the form of words and the order in which
words are usually arranged. Children learn this from their use of

language in talk, from hearing spoken language, and written language read aloud. It is this cue system which helps the reader to work out that the word was 'bed' rather than 'bolster' or 'banana'. It could be described, in simple terms, as the child's feel for the flow of language.

Children also use their knowledge of life and how the world works to make sense of a text. They read that the Bears were tired and that it was late, and so assume that they would be going to bed or to sleep rather than to work or to school. The cues based on the meaning of the text (semantic cue system) helped them make this decision. The picture of the bears going upstairs in their night clothes also gives an important clue. Children use their knowledge of books to help here; they know that the illustration, by definition, represents the meaning of the text, and so can be relied on to support their reading...

Finally children use their knowledge of printed letters and their relationship with the sounds of spoken language: the graphophonic cue system. It was this which enabled the child to know that the word was 'bed' rather than 'sleep'.

There are two important points to be made about the use of these four cue systems in helping children to make sense of a text.

The texts that help the reader

First it must be said that this particular text greatly facilitated the process. Not all texts offer such support. Some texts make it difficult for a reader to use the cue systems described here. A description of a child reading from a less sympathetic text will illustrate this possibility more closely.

Matt, aged five, had been in school for just half a term and had very recently been given his first 'reading book', Book 1a of the Ladybird *Key Words* reading scheme. He brought it to share with me, although the teacher had warned me, 'He knows nothing about reading at all.' After a general chat, Matt turned to the first page. On the right hand side was a picture of a young boy proudly holding a large football under his arm; on the left hand side was the word 'Peter'. Matt very carefully pointed to each letter in turn and read 'Peter plays with his ball.' What does this observation tell us about Matt as a reader?

● He knows how to open a book and where to begin to read.

- He knows the difference between the print and the picture.
- He knows that the print was the bit to read.
- He knows that each spoken word must correspond with a mark or set of marks with the page.
- He knows about pointing to the marks as the words are spoken.
- He knows that you read from left to right.
- He knows that the picture was related to what the print said.
- He knows that the language of books is different from his own spoken language.
- He knows that books often use the convention of the continuous present.
- He knows that the text often forms a caption to the picture.

Unlike his teacher, I think that Matt actually knows a lot about reading. His problem was that the text did not allow him to make use of what he already knew. Matt expected the text to have meaning, to tell a story, and to relate to the picture. In actual fact the text took the form of a caption and did not match Matt's experience of hearing books read to him.

This observation underlines the importance of the resources used in the classroom to help children to become readers. The work of Clark (1976 and 1988) and Ingham (1982) showed that children who become fluent enthusiastic readers are those who have had access to a wide variety of books and were encouraged from an early age to read for themselves, as well as being read to very frequently. Moira McKenzie (1986) describes what is required to enable children to become readers.

> A good reading and writing programme is embedded in a good learning context, within which teachers help children learn strategies that serve both their purpose in reading and the demands of the text being read. All readers ask implicit questions as they read. The basic ones are:
> does it make sense?
> does it sound like language?
> does it match with what I see?
> These questions build in self-monitoring and self-correction strategies. They can operate only in reading material that makes sense. (p.23)

Peace at Last made sense and so children can use what they already know to bring meaning to the text and take meaning from it. The book that Matt was reading did not support him in this; when he attempted to use his knowledge of language and books he did not succeed in decoding the text.

Selecting the strategy

The second point regarding the use of the cue systems in helping children make sense of the text is how we know which system to use when. It was possible to use a combination of the cue systems in reading the sentences from *Peace at Last*. These systems act together: an over-reliance on a single one will lead to ineffective reading. An effective reader is able to use all cue systems in order to synthesise the information that will enable him/her to make sense of the text. To return to Cameron's reading of *Bobby Brewster*, it can be seen that this is what his teacher was helping him to do. Cameron had learned an over-reliance on phonic analysis and so the teacher was encouraging him to use his knowledge of language and of life to make sense of the text. Throughout the reading Cameron's teacher was helping him to see that the text was carrying meaning and was a story to be enjoyed. She did this both by her own response to the story and by encouraging him to think about what would fit in with the sense of the story. She did not dismiss the graphophonic system entirely, though, and used it when appropriate, using Camerons' miscues as an indication of future teaching needs.

I have looked at the reading behaviour of a child who has made quite a start in the process of becoming a reader. I will now look at a younger child who is at the beginning of this process.

Wasim

Wasim was a reception child in his third term at school. He was reading a book from a published reading scheme (*The Oxford Reading Tree*) called *The Toy's Party*. He was reading it to an adult but the adult did not help him in any way. Wasim had been told to read the book by himself and when he was unsure of a word just to 'have a go'. The actual text of the book is given first in bold, followed by Wasim's reading of it. Wasim's first language is Punjabi and he is fairly fluent in English.

1 **Kipper wanted a party. Nobody wanted to come.**
The toy's party

2 **Nobody wanted to come.**
No come in the party.

3 **He got his toys.**
He got his toys. Here come the toys.

4 **He wanted a cake.**
Cake making. He made a cake.

5 **He put in cornflakes.**
He put in cornflakes.

6 **He put in tomato sauce.**
Put in the sauce, tomato sauce.

7 **He put in milk.**
Put it in the floor.

8 **He put in jam.**
Put it in the table.

9 **He put in sugar.**
Dog he cross. He no like that cake.

10 **He put in baked beans.**
He cross. The sauce in the cake.

11 **Mum was cross.**
Mum she cross.

12 **Kipper was sorry.**
Mum washing the teddy bear.

What does this transcript tell us about Wasim as a reader? Studying what he said alongside observations of him as he reads will help us to identify what he has learned already, what he will learn next and what kind of support for his learning he now needs.

Wasim made no attempt to point to the print while he was reading and it was not at all clear whether he was paying any attention to the print. Observation of him seemed to suggest that he was in fact 'reading' the pictures and relying on his own knowledge of the story to help him. Wasim certainly has a sense of story and there is some cohesion in his reading. The story flows and can be followed. Wasim even adds details, drawn from the illustrations, that have been omitted from the simplified text. This can be seen in lines 7, 8, 9 and 12.

Even when Wasim's reading does not match the printed words on the page, his 'reading' contains some perfect book style (line 3) and on many occasions is in perfect sentence form (lines 4 and 5, for example). Further experiences of listening to stories will give him support to continue to develop this ability.

I have previously mentioned the importance of the support given by the text itself; it is worth asking if this text actually helps Wasim in the process of becoming a reader. The text is very simple and repetitive, inevitable in a book written with a controlled vocabulary. This results in short and rather stilted sentences, which perhaps do not reflect the spoken language that Wasim has heard used at school and in his local environment. Yet he does generate a number of sentences that exactly fit this pattern, some of which match the printed text (lines 3 and 5) and some of which do not (lines 6, 7 and 8).

In terms of National Curriculum attainment targets Wasim is not yet operating at Level 1. However, he does show substantial understanding of what reading is, and of the nature of story; he has unquestionably begun the process of becoming a reader.

This leads me on to the question of assessment of children as readers, and, indeed, to consider the ways in which we choose to talk about learning to read and the reading process. The National Curriculum attainment targets cover a wide range of reading behaviours and have already been found not to be useful in describing children's understanding of the reading process. The description in the popular press, television and radio of children who had attained Level 1 in the S.A.T.s of 1991 as being 'unable to read' illustrated how the descriptions provided by S.E.A.C. are not adequate to describe this complex learning process. Several other attempts have been made to develop ways of recording children's progress as readers.

The I.L.E.A. *Primary Language Record* (1989) is widely known and used across the country. In its published form it is extensive and time-consuming to complete, although one can see the value of each aspect and it is hard to select areas to omit. The principles behind the design of the *Primary Language Record* are: the involvement of parents, the involvement of children, the involvement of all teachers who teach the child, the involvement of children with special educational needs, the importance of recording children's progress in the other community languages they know as well as English, the importance of recording developments across the curriculum in all major language modes, and the importance of a clear framework for evaluating language. The handbook to the record describes it in these words:

The new record offers a coherent view of what constitutes progress and development in language. It encourages teachers to identify children's strengths and note growth points, to regard errors as information, and to analyse patterns of error in a constructive way. It will be particularly helpful to teachers who are interested in informal methods of assessment, based on observation and on teacher judgment. (p.8)

It is not feasible to give a full analysis of the record here, but it is worth considering a little further the language that is used to describe children as readers. The notes on the record stress that reading is a process, and insist that children's reading must be thought of as located on a continuum moving from dependence to independence. However it is also considered important to take into account the quality of the reading experience rather than the number of books read.

Each term teachers are encouraged to collect a reading sample from each child, which enables them to make a detailed analysis, using informal assessment, miscue analysis or a running record. This serves to give a picture of each child's development and growing confidence with and access to strategies for sense making.

The principles of the *Primary Language Record* were commended in the Cox Report (1988) as a useful way of looking at children's reading and they tie in very well with the Programme of Study for reading, as it stands at the moment of writing. Many teachers have devised their own ways of exploring their children's reading but it must be said that the current climate of accountability requires more than a score on a reading test or a reading age, both of which give little information about a child's behaviour as a reader.

Much recent discussion about reading in primary classrooms has focussed on the 'teaching method' used and has polarised methods into 'reading schemes' versus 'real books'. I have already made the point that most teachers use a variety of methods and so in this discussion have tried to avoid this false division of approaches. Rather, in examining the reading behaviour of some young readers I have looked at the knowledge and attitudes they require to help them to make sense of a text. I can summarise this:

1 They need an expectation that the text will make sense and that they can make sense of it.

2 They need a knowledge of spoken language, not an explicit

knowledge but a practical working knowledge. Many children come to school with a great understanding of the grammatical patterns of English; others with less. All children need to have opportunities to talk and to listen.

3 They need a knowledge of books – of how they work, of the purpose and enjoyment of books and of that peculiar form of language that is found in books. We can never read too frequently or too much to children.

4 They need some understanding of how print works and of the relationships between letters and the sounds. Much of this is learned incidentally in the context of reading, but sometimes direct teaching is needed. Schemes such as Lyn Wendon's *Letterland* (1986) have been a highly popular way of doing this.

5 They need texts which help them to use what they already know and provide support for sense-making attempts, in the illustrations, the syntax and the layout.

Let us return to the question which forms the title of this chapter: How do children become readers? From observing the behaviour of children we can identify some factors that seem to play an important part in the process. I have listed some of those above. It must be made clear, however, that the ability to read does not just happen but that the supportive adult plays a crucial role. Look back and see how Cameron's teacher supported him and led him towards the appropriate strategy to use. In a completely different context, consider Beth's classroom, rich in stories, poems and jokes, and see how that helps children like Wasim to become familiar with the structures of English. The answer to the question is that we really do not know, but we can provide a context, resources and support which help children along the process of becoming readers.

CHAPTER FOUR

How do Children Become Writers?

Introduction

Let us start this chapter by looking at the National Curriculum documentation for English to see how writing is described there and what is considered important in the process of becoming a writer. There are three elements of writing in the Programme of Study for English: writing, spelling and handwriting. Three different attainment targets cover these areas. 'Writing' is defined as 'A growing ability to construct and convey meaning in written language matching style to audience and purpose.' We see therefore that, as in our present approaches to the teaching of reading, meaning is of central importance; the processes of reading and writing are thus intertwined.

Hall (1989) calls that part of writing concerned with constructing and conveying meaning, 'authorship' and defines it as 'the reflective generation of text (p.x). He goes on to describe how responsibility for a text is crucial in the emergence of authorship. The popular conception of an author is someone who has had work published and who therefore has probably completed more than one draft, refining and polishing ideas and style. However, a piece of writing does not start in that way. On a personal note, if you were to see my study as I write this you would see scribbled notes on pieces of paper of all shapes and sizes covering the desk and floor. I am writing this particular section in the middle of something which has already been written and no doubt it will be moved again before final publication. The whole business of writing, for me at least, tends to be rather messy and apparently unorganised; I hope, however, that the final product will not appear like that! The point that I am making, along with Hall, is that the task of 'authorship' is first and foremost one of conveying a message to an audience, about setting down ideas on paper. The tidying up of

Figure 4.1

that message for reading is only a part of the whole thing. If I have nothing to say, the ability to spell and write neatly is not much use to me. With this in mind, we shall now go on to look at some examples of writing from young children.

The first example (fig. 4.1) was dictated by a child to the teacher. The teacher wrote down the sentence and the child then copied underneath. What can we learn about this child as a writer? First, we can see that her letter formation is fairly accurate, although not having watched her write we do not know if she wrote from left to right in the correct sequence. We have some idea of her ability to construct a sentence but again do not know how much editing was done by the teacher. It is common for young children who are telling the teacher what they want to write to pour out a rich flow of language which perhaps might be rather untidy in its construction but which vividly conveys the excitement and adventure of, for example, a trip to the park. The teacher, aware of the young child's lack of skill in letter formation for under-copying, reduces this to 'I went to the park'. It is not long before the original richness of language becomes reduced to a similar formula each time. The children soon learn that this is what is acceptable for writing.

The development of spelling

The example quoted above tells us very little about the child as a writer. I went into a class of six-year-olds who had been introduced to only this form of writing and asked them to write for me with no help at all. Most children, after a little uncertainty, began to write. One little lad replied, 'I can't write words, only letters.' That comment in itself reveals much about his understanding of the forms of written language. I told the children that if they became stuck they could put a line and carry on. Some of the results below show a wide variety of competency with print and are useful to a teacher planning opportunities for future writing.

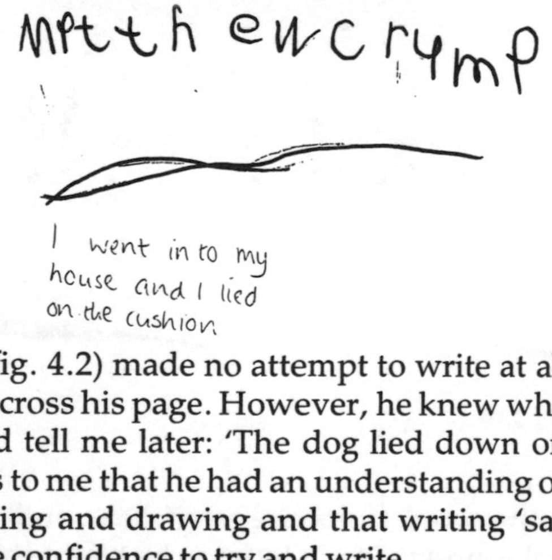

Mptth eNc rympp

I went in to my
house and I lied
on the cushion

Figure 4.2

Matthew (fig. 4.2) made no attempt to write at all but just put a straight line across his page. However, he knew what he wanted to say and could tell me later: 'The dog lied down on the cushion.' This indicates to me that he had an understanding of the difference between writing and drawing and that writing 'says' something, but lacked the confidence to try and write.

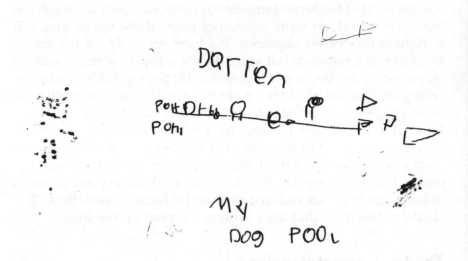

Figure 4.3

Darren's writing (fig. 4.3) used a mixture of recognisable letter shapes and some letter-like shapes, combining straight lines and open and closed curves. He wrote these from left to right across the page but it can be seen that he did not yet use word units. His writing 'says' 'I played with my dog'.

I went paddling down a stream

Figure 4.4

In figure 4.4 the word units are very clear and the child has written the initial sounds of each letter as he heard them. He wrote

'I was playing down a stream'. Note that 'I' is part of his sight vocabulary and also the use of 'u' for 'a'. He knows that there is more to come in each word for he has drawn a line, but the spaces between words are very clear.

Figure 4.5

Figure 4.5 reads as, 'I went on a nature walk'. This child has made an attempt to write using mainly his visual memory but aural memory is also involved. The letters 'wic' for 'walk' show how he has heard the first and last sounds of the word and recorded those according to his graphophonic knowledge. Other spellings bear a more tenuous relation to what he would hear and so he is relying on his visual memory e.g. 'weto' for 'went', 'nasvi' for 'for 'nature' and 'no' for 'on'.

In figure 4.6 we see that Sarah is making much more use of her phonic knowledge. She is writing as she hears words and using both letter names and sounds in her spelling, for example 'shy' and 'nys'. We can see that Sarah is beginning to realise that spelling is not always a simple letter-sound correlation as in the use of 'shy' instead of 'she'. She sees no inconsistency in using 'y' again to represent a completely different sound in 'nys' for 'nice'. However, Sarah's spelling of individual words is consistent (for example 'hur'), as is her use of particular letters for particular forms e.g. the consistent use of 'd' to indicate the past tense of verbs as in 'lfd', 'misd' and 'lvd'. Sarah is beginning to develop some pattern to her spelling. She has also used a complex sentence, with a verbal

When Miss Jackson
left I missed her
and I loved
her she was
nice.

Figure 4.6

clause of time. At an earlier stage she might have used a simpler construction, linking ideas by 'and'.

In the examples we can see the stages of development through which many children go in their spelling, as they approximate more and more closely to standard spellings over time. It is clear that learning to spell is a developmental process. Gentry (1987) identified four stages of spelling development, seeing spelling as a 'constructive developmental process' which he compared with the development of speech.

The first stage is pre-communicative spelling. Before this children scribble, as they play at writing, and then produce letter-like shapes. They then go on to use conventional letter shapes that do not have any relationship to sounds. Gentry describes children who write like this as 'spelling babblers'.

Children then move on to 'semi-phonetic' spelling where they realise that letters represent sounds but do not always represent all the sounds e.g. 'lvd' for 'loved' in Sarah's writing.

'Phonetic spelling' is the next stage where children write down exactly what they hear e.g. 'Jacsun' for 'Jackson'. They often achieve a systematic and quite sophisticated system for representing words in print.

'Transitional spelling' reflects the move from concrete to abstract representation and a greater reliance on visual memory than on writing words as they sound. Finally comes the stage of mature spelling when children and adults, on the whole, are able to spell according to convention.

In the above examples of children's writing several of these stages of spelling development can be seen and more are evident in the examples that follow. However, becoming a writer is not just a process of learning to spell conventionally and to form letters neatly; this view is reflected in the Programmes of Study and the attainment targets of the National Curriculum documentation for English. I will now consider the development of children's writing when they are allowed to behave as writers from the start.

Beginning writers

The next two case studies follow the development of two young children as writers. We shall look at their growth as authors as well as at the changes in their spelling, grammar and handwriting. They were both in the reception class described in chapter 1, of which Sue was the teacher. Sue allowed her class to behave as writers from the start and created a writing workshop ethos within her classroom. Her classroom might well be compared with the description given by Butler and Turbill (1984) in which they outlined five points that must be considered if teachers wish to create environments where learning to read and write are integrated into the whole process of language learning.

1 *Time*: to think, to talk, to revise and to complete.
2 *Ownership*: choices which are made by the children about the topic, the register and style, the purpose and the result of a piece of writing.
3 *Process*: recognition of the processes of rehearsal, drafting, revising and publishing.
4 *Conference*: support and guidance given to the writer.
5 *Resources*: a variety of reading material available.

Sue's classroom incorporated these key points.

Sophie

The first example of Sophie's writing was on her very first day in the reception class, aged five. She had come from the nursery of the school where she had been encouraged to write freely. Sophie

"my mum and dad
and me was going
up the park"

Sophie

Figure 4.7

came to the writing table in her new classroom where the teacher was sitting. She drew a picture and then wrote her story. She 'read' it to Sue who made a note later on of what Sophie's writing said. She had written 'My mum and dad and me was going up the park.' Figure 4.7 shows what Sophie's writing actually looked like.

What can we see that Sophie knows about writing? She is using recognisable letter shapes, many of which can be found in her name, and also some recognisable numeral shapes. She has written from left to right but has not made the distinction between word units. The clearer letter shapes in the first part of her writing suggests that perhaps she used what she knew and then wanted to write some more and so made up her own letters. However, we can only guess. We do know, though, that Sophie knows about the purpose of writing and is clearly using print to convey a message. Figure 4.8 shows what Sophie wrote some three weeks later.

She is now using only recognisable letter shapes. Perhaps Sophie's literacy experiences in school are teaching her that there are recognised, standardised and acceptable forms of print. There is still a clear tendency to concentrate on letters from her own name. It could be that this is the influence of her school reading experiences as later examples of her writing might illustrate.

the house with two

chimneys

Figure 4.8

Figure 4.9

Spaces between words are beginning to appear. The length of Sophie's writing, however, bears no relationship at all to what she is actually saying, which is: 'The house with two chimneys'.

Two weeks later figure 4.9 was written and this reflects quite a significant development in Sophie's growth as a writer. The translation is 'Me and my mummy seen a house and the council might let us live in it.'

The beginning of sound-symbol correspondence is clearly visible here and also Sophie's growing sight vocabulary; both of these have been influenced by her reading experiences. Note the mnemonic drawings which the teacher used to draw to help children to remember the word 'look' and which Sophie also uses. The word 'look' however is not in what Sophie is actually saying but there is a very strong semantic link with the word 'seen'. It is also interesting to note that Sophie is quite happy to use two different sound of 'y' in 'my' and 'mummy'; she is already aware of the inconsistencies of the English spelling system.

The next example (fig. 4.10) was written a month later and the teacher responds by writing a question. Sophie wrote, 'The little girl is going outside to play in the sunshine.'

Sophie is now using a much greater variety of letters, which are

Figure 4.10

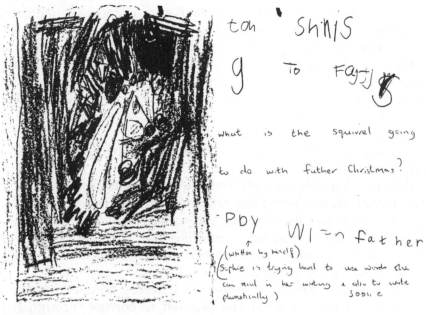

tan `shnis

g To Fayrts

what is the squirrel going

to do with futher Christmas?

PDY Wl=n father

(written by herself)

(Sophie is trying hard to use words she
can read in her writing & also to write
phonetically)   Sophie

Figure 4.11

the lie t g is

g to the hienk

why, is the little girl

going to the house?

B cki oll the

B nok

"Because of the big dog"

Sophie?

monday 25

Figure 4.12

mostly correctly formed, although there are some reversals. Notice the copyright sign at the end of her writing. The teacher had been discussing this in a shared reading session and several children then started putting it on their work as a sign of ownership. You will also see that the teacher responded to Sophie's work by writing a question at the end. By doing this she was responding as a reader to the meaning of the writing and also providing a model for correct transcription. Sophie used the question in her response; not as something to copy but as a resource.

Three weeks later Sophie wrote figure 4.11 'The squirrel is going to Father Christmas's'.

We can see in this example that the word units are quite clearly marked and there is now beginning to be a closer link between the letters written and the message the writing conveys. Sophie has used her visual memory for words like 'the', 'to' and 'is' and has made use of the initial sound to represent words as in 'snn' for 'squirrel' and 'g' for 'going'.

The teacher's written question now serves another purpose, reminding Sophie of what she wanted to convey through her writing, without giving Sophie the message that her writing is wrong. Sophie uses it as a resource for writing her reply, and also uses words she has come across in her reading e.g. 'pay' for 'play'. Sophie is now behaving as a real writer in the way she communicates with and responds to her reader.

The next example was written three weeks later. 'The little girl is going to the house... Because of the big dog' (fig. 4.12).

This piece of writing is even more readable. Sophie is getting closer and closer to convention. She is also able to convey a message through her writing and there is a real development from the early examples which were just labelling of the contents of the picture, to labelling which is a description of an action.

Sophie's use of her sight vocabulary is now evident: 'the', 'is', 'to'. She represents the strongest sounds in words, leaving out others e.g. 'lle' for 'little'. She still uses initial letters to represent whole words, and, in this example, uses the same letter for two different words: 'girl' and 'going'. She starts the word 'house' with the appropriate initial sound and then goes on to use an apparently random string of letters. In her reply we can see the first appropriate use of upper case letters. It is interesting however to see that Sophie has not used the teacher's question as a resource but has replied to the question in a very appropriate manner.

Figure 4.13

My last example was written six weeks later and the Christmas holiday has come in between. Sophie wanted to convey a very important message in this piece of writing and does so most effectively. 'My birthday is on fireworks night.' (fig. 4.13).

She has used her sight vocabulary ('is', 'my' and 'on') and also the resources of the classroom from which she has copied the word 'fireworks'. She is using her phonic knowledge to make informed attempts at the spelling of other works and her attempts are very close to the correct version. Note however her use of letter names at times instead of letter sounds e.g. 'bfda' for birthday and 'nit' for night. Sophie has communicated most effectively in this piece of writing; she uses language appropriately for her purpose of communicating a vital piece of information and is in full control of her writing. Sophie has learned to behave as an author.

Sophie's development as a writer over the six months we have observed has reflected many influences: her reading and the classroom environment, her growing knowledge of letters and her sense of an interested audience which was responsive to her writing. The examples shown here are only a few of the many pieces of writing that Sophie did during this time. They were chosen to show the development that took place in the process of Sophie becoming a writer. I make no claim that Sophie has arrived at the end of her journey towards becoming a writer; she still has some way to go. However, she had made a very positive start and appears to be growing confident in her use of written language.

Andy

Andy was also a member of Sue's class and had spent the same amount of time in the same nursery as Sophie. As I look at his development as a writer it can be seen that his progress was not quite so rapid and apparent and yet it is clear that he also was learning about writing and what it means to be an author. Some other influences on his writing can also be seen; Andy was a great fan of video cartoons.

The first example (fig. 4.14) was written on his first day in the reception class. He wrote, 'The pirates ate the gold'. Andy knew that there is a clear distinction between writing and drawing and the two can be distinguished in his work. He begins by using some of the letters from his name and then goes on to 'play writing'. Here Andy is imitating the form of adult writing as it appears to him, although he used no recognisable letter shapes. However, he is clearly acting as an author in that he has created a text which contains a story.

Figure 4.14

"the fox has got teeth and hes eting his legs"

Figure 4.15

robot

the boy whipped the boy down.

Figure 4.16

The next example (fig. 4.15) was written three weeks later and says, 'The fox has got teeth and he's eating his legs.' There is clear indication in this writing that Andy has moved on in his development as a writer. He is now using recognisable letter shapes which shows a growing realisation that there is a convention of mark making on paper. The content of Andy's writing is still very context bound; he has not yet realised that writing needs to be fully explicit and his story does not have cohesion – we are not sure whose legs the fox is eating!

Two weeks later Andy wrote figure 4.16 which, he told his teacher, says, 'The boy whipped the boy down.' Andy has learned yet more about writing. He knows that it says something and he knows that it takes particular forms. Here Andy used the chart of the days of the week, displayed in the classroom as a learning aid and resource. However, he used it to say what he wanted to say which had nothing whatever to do with the days of the week! Andy has learned that there are conventions for writing, that there are ways of making marks on the paper that enable people to read what you have read. Andy took private ownership of this public print and appropriated it for his own purposes.

Three weeks later he wrote, 'Mrs Mills is going to see the witch to

Mrs mills is going to see the witch to see a little log to buy him

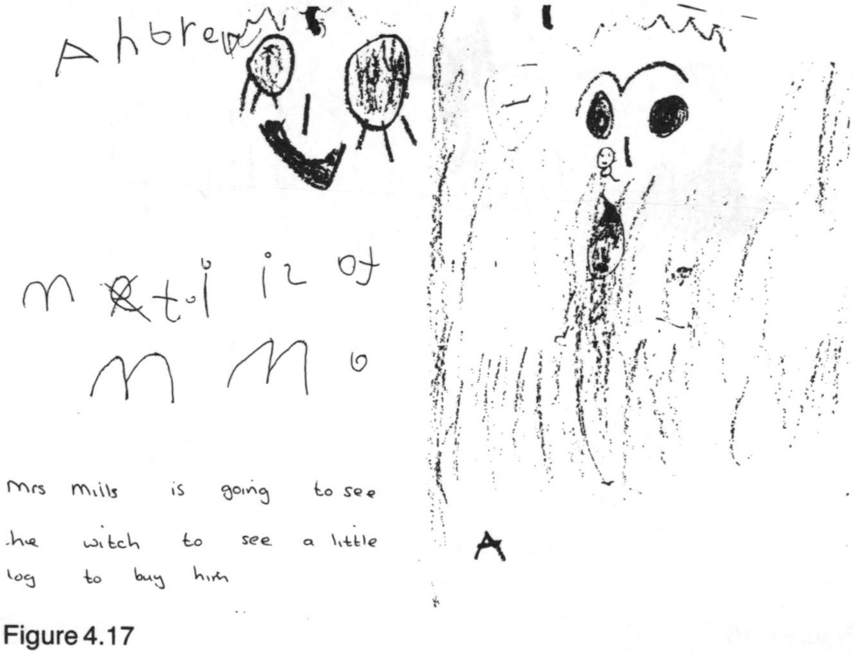

Figure 4.17

ISAb re
WNb— aBh
US mga

thira UP¡t 5

What happened to the chocolate?
Si whb

I hope he enjoyed it!

Figure 4.18

LeisWNs
AnBBW

What a beautiful diamond.
Did you find it in the
mud?
reb

Figure 4.19

see a little dog to buy him.' (fig. 4.17). Here is the first example of sound-symbol correlation in the use of the letter 'm'. Andy is not using it in a way that can be directly matched to a specific word but he seems to be aware that the sound occurs several times in what he wants to say and that it can be represented by that particular shape.

We can also see the beginnings of the use of a sight vocabulary e.g. 'is' and 'to'. This could be the influence of Andy's literacy experiences in school. These experiences included frequent times of shared writing, where the teacher and a group of children would together compose a text, with the teacher acting as scribe on a large piece of paper. It may well be that from these experiences Andy has also learned that it is all right to cross out errors. Note as well Andy's use of the full stop, in the enclosed circular form – he is obviously becoming aware of all features of print!

There is a significant change in the content of Andy's writing. This can be read alone by Andy and will make sense. It is also the first time Andy has written about an actual person, the nursery nurse in his class, and a real event, going to visit, although it is still intertwined with fantasy.

A month later figure 4.18 was written, which says 'I saw boy with a big bar of chocolate... He ate it.' Andy seems now to have more confidence in his use of print and is able to take control of it for himself. He uses recognisable letter shapes and the beginnings of word units are distinguishable. He is using a mixture of upper and lower case letters.

The teacher responded to this piece of Andy's writing by writing a question, as she had done with Sophie. Andy replies using some of the letters from the teacher's writing but not all. Note also the way he has used the question mark; it could be that Andy is not able to distinguish between that and another letter shape or it could be that he sees it as a mark which is used in a question and answer sequence – we are not able to tell. What is significant is that Andy is using writing in order to communicate.

Two weeks later Andy wrote 'I found a beautiful diamond.' (fig. 4.19). It might be considered that Andy has made little progress in his writing development; there are no word units apparent and there is no connection between the letters used and the meaning they convey. However, children need time to consolidate what they have learned and it could be that this is what Andy has been

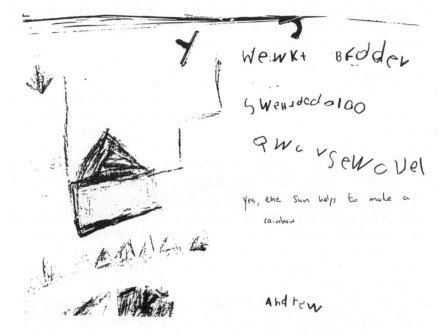

Figure 4.20

doing. He does, however, respond appropriately to the teacher's question with an approximation to the word 'Yes', which must come from his sight vocabulary.

The last example of Andy's writing comes several weeks later after the Christmas break. Figure 4.20 reads 'When the sun shines there is a rainbow.' Here there is clear demarcation of word units, the use of recognisable letter shapes in both upper and lower case but no sound-symbol correlation.

Andy still has a long way to go in learning the conventions of written language but he has come a long way already. However, he is still able to behave as an author, generating text and communicating and responding to meaning. It seems that Andy has learned something of textual cohesion and has also developed a sense of audience.

In both Sophie and Andy's writing the influence of the teacher's programme and aspects of the classroom environment is clear. Let us spend time looking at some of those influences.

Hall (1987) describes three aspects of classrooms which are critical if the 'emergence of literacy is to be continuous' (p.82). He advocates an environment where literacy has a high profile and status, where there is access to valid demonstrations of literacy and opportunities to engage in purposeful literacy acts, which are acknowledged as valid literacy behaviour.

1. *The literate environment of the classroom*

I have discussed the way in which young children are surrounded by print in a variety of forms, being used in a variety of ways, before they come to school. The classroom is also a print environment and as teachers we need to consider the forms and functions of print that children see there, to ensure that they build on children's existing understandings and experiences, especially when the classroom contains bilingual children.

The difference between school literacy and other forms of literacy has been made clear in earlier chapters but it is still possible to allow children to use and build on what they already know. The environment of the classroom can go a long way towards enabling children to do this.

Sophie and Andy's classroom did in fact give a high profile to literacy. We can go round the room looking at the messages that were conveyed through the environment.

Just outside the door was a board displaying messages for parents; this told them the topic that the children were working on that week, reminded them of forthcoming events and passed on special pieces of news. Just inside the classroom door was another board on which the teacher and nursery nurse put reminders to themselves about children going home early, visitors to the classroom, etc. Here children were seeing writing as a way of creating permanent reminders and as a way of passing on information.

The book corner of the room was large and comfortably furnished with a bench and cushions. The books were well displayed and easily accessible to the children who were encouraged to use the book corner frequently. Browsing was seen as a positive and valuable way of spending time, and the adults regularly made this value explicit in their talk with parents and children.

The display in the classroom was both teacher-and child-initiated and invited the children to respond. On one occasion a child bought in an empty food packet from home, very excited at having discovered a word on it. The teacher spent some time with the class talking about this and encouraging other children to look for words and bring examples in. The result was a display board full of different forms and functions of print, which became a valued source for much learning.

The home corner contained examples of printed materials which would be found in many homes e.g. newspapers and magazines, telephone directories, shopping lists, junk mail and much more. Children were using these as a part of their play, which thus provided opportunities for literacy learning.

There was a writing trolley containing a variety of materials which children could use to write, including an old typewriter. Children were encouraged to go there at any time to write.

Other areas of the classroom reflected written material as a way of recording ideas and the different ways were discussed. A powerful example of this was the music area. It contained several instruments – both tuned and untuned – and quite a few music books and cards on which were written the words and musical notation of the children's favourite songs. The children would go and play and sing these songs as they 'read' the music. Some children also composed their own music to songs and then wrote it down using musical notation.

These are descriptions of selected parts of the classroom showing that literacy had a high profile. The way in which literacy was an integral part of the environment made it possible for children to read and write easily and naturally.

2. *Demonstrations of literacy*

I now go on to consider the sort of literacy activities that took place in the classroom where Sophie and Andy were learning. Too often in schools any literacy behaviour, particularly perhaps writing, is done by the pupils to please the teacher. It may be perceived as an end in itself, rather than as a purposeful and meaningful activity in its own right. The old joke of one child saying to another, 'Don't look out of the window or she'll make you write about it,' is too true for comfort. It can also be said that in many classrooms children rarely see adults reading or writing and getting pleasure from it.

Mention has already been made of the notice boards inside and outside Sue's classroom door where messages were left for the parents, and for the children and adults within the classroom. The children also made use of these boards and saw the messages being read and written, often taking an active role in the latter.

Many teachers are now reading alongside their class in E.R.I.C. time (Everybody Reading In Class), also known as S.S.R. (Sustained Silent Reading). Fewer have yet started to write alongside the children as they write. Doing this can provide children with a powerful demonstration of the writing process, showing them that it is all right to cross out, change your mind, move pieces of text around and re-read what you have written.

The activity of shared writing can make this process overt and allows the teacher to guide the children through a variety of acts. This approach is based on the principle of Vygotsky that what a child can do in cooperation today she can do alone tomorrow. In shared writing a group of children and the teacher compose together; the teacher acts as scribe on a large sheet of paper but the children are the authors. This offers opportunities for teaching many different aspects of the writing process from specific teaching points, for example spelling patterns or punctuation, to larger questions of audience, style and register.

Writing by the teacher is an important part of the day-to-day running of a classroom and yet it is often done surreptitiously and without the children being aware of what is going on. Involving the children in routines such as taking the register and sending messages to other teachers can show them something of the purposes of literacy and avoid the danger of their seeing writing in school as being always an end in itself. I was once in a classroom observing and taking field notes; I would move around the classroom sitting with the children and scribbling rough notes in a small notebook I carried with me. I noticed that a child was also moving around the room writing on a piece of paper which she had folded into a book shape. I asked what she was doing and the reply was, 'I'm doing what you're doing – writing down what all the children do.' Such is the power of the behaviour of adults in the class as models!

3. *Engagement in Literacy*

Hall (1987) says that children need opportunities to engage in 'purposeful literacy acts which are acknowledged as valid literacy behaviour'. As teachers we need to consider the kinds of writing we ask children to do, to ensure that we do not fall into that all-to-easy routine of 'Draw a picture and write about it', which can follow every school event. The way in which we structure our classrooms and the extent to which we give the children choices about their writing is important here.

Sue's practice of asking the children written questions about their writing was one way of encouraging them to write with a purpose. With older children, this written dialogue can be extended in semi-private journals. An extension of this is letter writing; the children can exchange letters with another school or class, write away for information about a particular topic they are covering, or write to their parents informing them of forthcoming school events. Writing and publishing books for younger children can also give writing a real purpose and genuine audience.

The context of the classroom can also create opportunities for 'real' writing in play. I have already discussed the way in which a home corner can be made 'literate'; making a restaurant, an office, a hospital, or a shop can also enable the children to engage in 'real' writing which is both like that of the world outside school, and an integral part of their play. As teachers we need to ensure that these pieces of writing are accepted and valued in the classroom as much as others.

I return to the question which forms the title of this chapter: 'How do children become writers?' In examining the growth of Sophie and Andy we have seen how the skills of transcription and authorship grow alongside each other. In a classroom where opportunities for writing in many different forms are given, where children's writing behaviours are accepted and valued for what they are, where children see examples of writing for many different purposes, writing becomes an integral part of day-to-day life. In this way children are acknowledged as writers from the start and then given the skills and understanding necessary to learn more. Meanwhile, it must not be forgotten that listening to and reading a wide variety of texts will also be a rich resource for the developing author.

CHAPTER FIVE

Moving On

Darren

I want to begin this chapter with the story of Darren, a Year 6 pupil in a large suburban primary school. Darren hated reading. He had gone through primary school avoiding books and reading as little as possible. However, when I spoke to Darren in the second term of his final year he was changing. Let Darren tell his own story; what follows is the transcript of Darren talking to me about himself as a reader.

There's a teacher who helps people who are having troubles with reading. I went to her because I couldn't pronounce different words. I didn't like reading because of the books. In the lower school you had to read schemes which were boring. I didn't like to read them and so I didn't have much practice.

Did you always find reading difficult?

No, I learned very easily. When I was little I was good at reading. In the reception class we had number cards and words on cards. You had to learn them at home, then you went on to the reading scheme. That goes on for a very long time. Lots of my friends used to skip a few pages but I never did because it's important to read the whole thing if the teacher gives you a book to read.

What put you off reading?

The style of the books was very boring. They had things in them like 'Grandma knitted James a new scarf'. I wasn't really interested in that and so I didn't do very well. I knew that I wasn't good and that put me off as well. I didn't practise and so I didn't get any better.

What happened to change that?

When I got into Year 6, for the first weekend's homework Miss M.. told us to read a book – any book. I had a book by Roald Dahl at home and so I read that. Now I can't get enough of them.'

What do you like about Roald Dahl's writing?
   The style of writing – I think he's a very good writer. He tells the story well.
It's hard to describe but I like the plot of his books. A lot of children like him.
Do you read any other books?
   No – only Roald Dahl.

This account raises several issues worth considering. The way
in which Darren's attitude to reading changed through the course
of his primary schooling is not untypical, and maybe we can learn
from it.

First, why did he lose interest in reading? There are several
answers, which Darren himself gives. The main problem seems to
be the books which he was required to read and which Darren saw
as boring. The plots were unexciting and did not inspire him to
read further. Darren had no sense of purpose; he describes the
scheme as carrying on 'for a very long time'. For Darren reading
was a matter of ploughing your way through a long series of boring
books and this caused him to lose heart. He had no choice about the
books he was given to read and his interest and motivation seemed
to play no part in the reading programme. Finally Darren felt that
reading was all about being right or wrong, and as he said himself,
'I couldn't do it.' There is little motivation to continue when you see
yourself as a constant failure.

Second, we may ask: how did Darren understand the process of
reading? The language he uses to describe it is revealing. He uses
words and phrases such as: sounding out, pronunciation, practice,
repetition, unending. It seems that Darren saw reading as an ever-
lasting teacher-controlled programme through which pupils had to
work. His role was to do as the teacher said and soldier on through
the series of books. The fact that these books held no interest for
him resulted in slow progress and an increasing lack of motivation. It may well be that Darren's teachers throughout the primary
school would be surprised to know how Darren viewed reading,
and yet, as Margaret Meek says (1982) '...our pupils' views of what
learning to read means may have very little in common with our
own.'

A picture is being created of a little boy who saw reading as
something which he would be taught to do at school and who had
little reading experience at home. He hoped that if he just did what
the teacher told him he would learn to read. However, he soon lost
interest, and did not have either the experience, motivation or

nerve to break out and do his own thing as he felt some of the other children were doing. So he stumbled on, his progress becoming slower and slower and yet not able to break away from the system which in itself was killing his interest and motivation.

If we go on to ask ourselves what it was that changed Darren's attitude to reading, we can see that it was the teacher in his final year of primary school. Darren was still struggling through the scheme, part of a group of children who had difficulties with reading, and had been given yet more scheme books to read. However the teacher chose to overlook this fact and gave responsibility for his reading back to Darren. The task of reading a book over that first weekend did several things for him.

It gave the ownership of his reading to Darren himself. He was told that he could read anything he wanted, and it would be accepted as valid. The choice was his own, completely unencumbered by any notion of suitability of the book. In addition, the weekend task offered Darren privacy for his reading. It was not made a public performance where his inadequacies would be on display; he was required to read the book to himself at home, where it would not matter if could not read every word. This task immediately changed the emphasis from decoding every single word to enjoyment of the chosen book. Lastly, the book which Darren chose was exciting to him, and one which captured his interest.

Darren has by no means reached the end of the line in his development as an enthusiastic and competent reader. He is still only reading books by Roald Dahl and it is worth considering how Darren might be helped to extend his reading repertoire. One could encourage him to read books of a similar genre or with similar themes, or ask him to compare the writing of Roald Dahl with the work of another author. Whatever strategy is adopted, careful handling is required to ensure that Darren does not lose his new-found enthusiasm for reading and that his ownership of his reading is not taken away from him once more.

Helping those who struggle

The story of Darren is by no means untypical of children at this stage in their schooling. Martin (1989) gives a moving transcript of a conversation with Leslie about his self-perceived reading failure. There are many echoes with Darren's experiences. Martin goes on to make four points, which we as teachers need to remember when we come across children such as these.

First, we need to be aware of their histories. Such children have had many experiences of continued failure; for them reading is far from being a pleasurable experience. They have frequently met well-intentioned adults who tried method after method without success; this experience often results in a hardened cynicism in the children.

Martin's second point is that we need to recognise the strong emotions engendered by reading in these children. Leslie did not like the extra times teachers heard him read because he felt that these highlighted his failure; Darren began to enjoy reading when he was given the chance to read by himself, without any sense of public performance increasing his feeling of inadequacy. Darren's teacher managed to achieve that fine balance between compulsion and encouragement.

Third, Martin reminds us that many different methods had been used with Leslie in an attempt to teach him to read, and yet all had failed. As teachers we need to recognise that the answer may not lie in the teaching methods, but in the extent to which the learner's energy and motivation can be brought to bear on the task. What is essential is that children are infected with the enthusiasm and motivation for reading that will enable them to enter into the world of books.

Finally, Martin says, we need to be aware of the view of reading that we are conveying to children. Often we spend a great deal of time helping children to learn to read, without giving them regular, sustained opportunities to do any reading in school. We talk about the pleasure which can be gained from reading and yet children never see us reading for pleasure. We tell them about the exciting books that are available and yet our classroom book areas are small and contain old, tatty and uninspiring books. The point is that the context of literacy learning carries as strong, if not stronger, messages about literacy as our actual teaching programme.

Mature readers

Holdaway (1980) gives a useful description of a mature literacy user. He says,

> The outstanding feature of mature literacy is the unique relationship it displays in the lives of individuals. It has no convergent form or upper limit, but rather constitutes a

body of learning strategies which allow the mature reader to extend and develop new skills or refinements of skill to meet changing life purposes. It often becomes inter-est-and-vocation-centred. Rapid comprehension tends to develop first in areas of habitual preoccupation served by highly-refined powers of prediction which are based on knowledge and familiarity. (p. 30)

Let us now look at a teacher talking with some Year 4 children about their reading and consider how she is helping them to become mature readers.

Rachel, aged nine, was reading *The Ghost of Thomas Kemp* by Penelope Lively.

T: What've you thought about this book so far?

R: It's quite exciting.

T: What's it mainly about?

R: Um. I can't say it – there's a kind of ghost.

T: Like a poltergeist?

R: Yes. And this exorcist comes to get rid of it.

T: What was a bit unusual about the exorcist? Was it what you would've expected? What was his real job?

R: He was a builder.

T: Yes. I wouldn't expect an exorcist to be a builder in real life, would you, but a vicar or something like that.

R: He did mention vicars – he said that vicars were very good to get rid of them.

In this short excerpt the teacher was helping Rachel to relate the story she was reading to life. By discussing what is surprising in the text she is showing Rachel that it is a positive thing to bring your own expectations and understandings to a book. The inter-action between these and the text creates the meaning which the book holds for you on that particular reading. Rachel is learning that reading is an active involvement with a text.

Luke, aged eight, had been struggling with a book and after several attempts had decided to abandon it. In her comments the teacher shows him that this is perfectly acceptable behaviour, and that such judgements are ones which mature readers are able to make.

T: Now Luke, you decided not to read *Mike and Me* any more. Why did you decide? What was the reason? I said to you to go back and read the first four chapters again, didn't I because you didn't remember a word of it, did you? Why do you think you didn't remember it? Were you really enjoying the story?

L: No.

T: And because of that you really didn't want to carry on, did you?

L: No.

T: I think it wasn't really a very suitable book for you, was it? There's nothing wrong with that. We just change our minds – like all sorts of things. So you decided to have *Please Mrs Butler* and you tell me you haven't read any of these before.

It is tempting to think from this extract that the teacher was doing a little too much of the talking, asking too many closed questions, and not allowing Luke to get a word in edgeways. However, it is important to put the whole thing into context. Luke had been struggling with his reading to date. Rather like Darren, he was a child who plodded mechanically through his reading books without any real involvement or enjoyment. His teacher had pushed him to take responsibility for his own reading by making him take decisions about what he would read and was now trying to show him that this responsibility was real, and that the decisions he had made were valid and accepted. The teacher attempts to show Luke that reading is another activity very much like the other activities in his life which he enjoys and in which he takes an active role. So often children see reading as some sort of mysterious pursuit related only to school, having very little connection with the world outside the classroom.

In this next conversation the teacher is giving Matt some insight into the world of authors, helping him to see them as real people.

T: Right, Matt. You've chosen this time a book that's a bit different. The last book that you read was a poetry book and the one before that was a book about birds. This time you've chosen a book that's really quite an easy one for you to read. Why have you chosen this one? Just for a bit of fun? It's Roger McGough, *The Stowaways*.

M: I thought it looked good.

T: And knowing Roger McGough as well you thought it could be quite a funny one. Have you read any other Roger McGough books?

M: *(thoughtfully but with some uncertainty)* I don't think so.

T: But you've seen bits and pieces. Where did we see him? Can you remember where we saw him? On the 'Picture Box' programmes. Roger McGough used to present those – the one with the glasses.

M: *(with surprise)* Oh.

T: Did you not realise that? Right, I know that you saw this book when Luke brought it into school and so I said that you could read it.

M: *(in excitement)* I didn't know it was him.

Matt is an extremely able and fluent reader and, as is mentioned in this extract, chooses to read a variety of texts. Matt is also a very reticent child and finds it hard to express his opinions and ideas publicly; this appears to be because he is afraid of making mistakes. Matt's teacher told me that she was trying to encourage him to be bolder in his choices. It is clear that the teacher is creating within her classroom an atmosphere of sharing and talking about books, since Matt first came across this book when a friend of his brought it in from home and talked about it enthusiastically in the classroom.

The teacher is here talking with Matt about the author of the book and creating a picture of a person whom Matt has seen in other contexts, who also happens to write books. She is showing Matt that one can use what one knows about the author in order to make judgements about a book and to inform future choices. It is clear from Matt's reaction that the author of a book had not really paid a part in his choice of book before and that this is a new and interesting aspect to consider. The transcript does not really convey the surprise, interest and curiosity which come over on the tape.

Knowing about authors is something which can not only help children in their reading but can also give them added interest and motivation as writers, as we will discuss later in this chapter.

The final extract shows the teacher discussing with Judith a poem which she had just read. The poem was 'The Broken Toys', from the collection *Is a Caterpillar ticklish?*

T: So what's this poem all about Judith?

J: It's someone's toys in their bedroom.

T: Yes. And what sort of state are all these toys in?

J: In a mess.

T: What's happened to them basically?

J: Well, the doll's eyes are all out and the dolls' house has been tipped upside down and the toys are rusty.

T: What are some of the words in the poem to say what the toys are like?

J: They've got battered and tattered.

T: Yes. What does that mean?

J: Well battered means it can be smashed.

T: What about tattered?

J: It's like it's in rags.

T: That's right and what about the – what's happened to the tin tea set?

J: It's buckled and bent.

T: What does it mean to be buckled?

J: Is it kind of – buckled?

T: Twisted, mis-shapen – the shape's gone – it's been bent out of shape and all these toys are – basically they're – what's one word to describe all the toys?

J: They are..

T: One word they keep using in the poem and it's in the title as well.

J: The broken toys.

T: They're broken, aren't they – broken and dusty. So the man in the poem describes it and he feels a bit sad about them. How do you know that? What word does he use that means sort of sad?

J: Um.

T: This word forlorn means sort of sad and neglected. You can imagine this big heap of toys in a corner can't you? Nobody plays with them, nobody cares about them anymore. In the broken box the broken toys – sad, forlorn – they're a bit neglected.

On first reading this again seems a classic example of the teacher talking too much, asking too many closed questions and not giving the child a chance to say much. Let us look a little closer and see what is actually happening here.

The teacher talks about specific words used in the poem and discusses them to ensure that Judith has understood what is being said. In building up shared meanings for these words they are recreating the atmosphere of the poem and the description of the toys. Through this rather prescriptive conversation the teacher is attempting to extend Judith's vocabulary and to help her see how words can be used together to create a mood.

The National Curriculum documentation requires that children are able to 'read a range of material with some independence, fluency, accuracy and understanding.' The extracts given above show how much is implied in learning these skills and how important the context of learning is in determining what will best help individual children. As discussed earlier in this book, both the classroom context and the teacher's understanding of literacy will have a substantial effect on children's view both of literacy and of themselves as readers and writers.

As children develop as readers and writers the need for them to see literacy, their literacy, as an essential part of day-to-day life continues to be of central importance. The comments of Leslie and Darren suggest that they saw literacy as something done by pupils in schools in order to satisfy and please teachers. If satisfying and pleasing the teacher does not have a high priority in one's thinking, one would be justified in thinking there is little point in reading or writing. The relationship between literacy and learning is very close and the two processes affect each other both in the classroom and generally. In the following chapter I shall look at some different examples of writing for learning; here I shall consider some examples where it could be said that literacy is used as a basis for learning.

Literacy and learning

During a visit to an industrial museum, Judith's class visited a working mine. Some of them, inspired by their own reading of poetry, chose to write about their visit in poetic form. The teacher took this opportunity to generate talk about the feelings that had been generated by the visit and their discussion of working life at that time. She encouraged the children to empathise with children of the period and to express this feeling in their writing. Two examples follow.

Letitia was impressed by two aspects of what she had learned: the young age of the children working in the mine, and the danger of life in the mines. She wanted to convey both ideas in writing. Her first draft reads as follows:

I was only seven when I had to go do down for the first time. The cage that I had to go down was judder and shudder and suddenly I just feared for my life.

The cave was slimy and sharp. I hard a faint noise but when I got closer it was some one singing. I could not see them because of the dark.

I heard a rumbull then the roof fell on me.

In this first attempt Letitia was primarily concerned with sorting out what she wanted to say and the feelings she wished to convey. She is not particularly concerned with the form or style of her writing. She is only just beginning to plan the structure of her poem and the flow of events and feelings. The second draft is:

I was only seven when I got in the cage. It juddered and shuddered. I feared for my life.

The cave was slimy and sharp. I heard a faint noise but when I got closer it sounded louder. Then suddenly the roof fell in.

Here Letitia has cut out all superfluous wording and kept her writing to the bare minimum in order to convey the intensity of feeling. She has retained some literary sounding language, for example, 'I feared for my life.' The omission of the person singing serves to highlight the feeling of loneliness, isolation and fear and gives more impact to the final sentence. In the final draft she did not alter the words or phrases used in the second draft, but worked on the layout of the poem, in order to give it more obviously 'poem-like' structure, and an increased momentum towards the final catastrophe. Letitia told me that she kept on reading her poem aloud at this stage to help her to see where the pauses should come

I was only seven when
I got in the cage.
It juddered
and shuddered.
I feared for my life.

The cave was
slimy and sharp.
I heard a faint noise but
when I got closer it sounded
louder

Then
suddenly
the roof fell in.

Letitia has used the technique of writing lines of single words, in order to give them more impact and I believe that in this case she is fairly successful.

In using a poem to write about her experience of the visit, Letitia was helped to a greater historical understanding of what life was really like at the time. In writing her poem she was thinking about her feelings and emotions and so for her the knowledge gained through the visit became alive in a way it might not have done if her writing had been a purely factual account.

Another pupil, Kate, also wrote a poem about this same visit. I have only the final draft and yet it is well worth reproducing here because I think that it shows how the process of writing has fostered her dramatic and emotional understanding.

Mining for Death
I can hear the dark calling me,
As I climb into the shaft,
Down in to the depth of the earth.
The cage trembles as I go down,
It feels like death is touching me
Like icy fingers on my hand.
Then out of the never-ending darkness
I hear an explosion from below.
Another person will never see the dawn.
As I get lower the dark seems to come over me,
And I am swallowed up in the realms of darkness.

In the previous chapter we looked at two young children at the beginning stage of becoming writers. Looking at some examples of the writing of older children will help us to see how they can be helped to write in different ways and for different audiences. The last two examples showed how writing can be used in different curriculum areas. These examples show how the process of writing can help children come to an understanding of concepts and attitudes and how written language can be used and manipulated to convey ideas. That is what Letitia and Kate were doing through the writing of their poems although of course other forms of learning were going on as well.

Drafting

Some Year 3 children were just beginning to revise their writing independently. Some of them did this with other members of the class, some still needed to talk through their work with the teacher and some responded to questions the teacher had written on their writing. I reproduce here just the first two drafts of a piece of writing by one child where she was looking at the content rather than aspects of presentation. The class had been reading and comparing Aesop and Terry Jones's fairy tales. Some of the children then decided to write their own fairy tales. Rachel's story was called 'Two Men'. The drafts are reproduced using the spelling and punctuation with which they were written.

Draft 1
Once upon a time there was a man and he worked in a Bun shop and the

man first had one castemer who bought 15 currnt buns and 12 Dough-nuts then another man came along and bought 2 carrnt buns and one doughnut.

After writing this Rachel gave her work to the teacher who read and responded by writing questions on the end. Rachel wrote the answers to these questions.

What happened then? The man went home who had less.
Did the man who bought the most eat them all? Yes but as the other man was going home he caught him and ate the doughnuts.
What did the man who only bought 3 cakes do? ran home.

Rachel then wrote a second draft.

Once upon a time there was a man and he worked in a Bun shop and the man first had one customer who bought 15 current buns and 12 doughnuts. Then another man came along and bought 2 current buns and one dough-nut. Then the man who had less went home and the man who had more caught the other man and ate his buns and the other man's buns and then ran home.

In this rather confusing story Rachel was exploring the idea of greed and the feeling that she had that those who have more material possessions seem to take even the little that the poor have. This is quite a profound concept for an eight-year-old child to understand and express in terms relevant to her own experiences. In discussing the idea and creating the written story, she was learning how to make ideas clear to the reader. She still has quite a bit of learning to do!

The teacher was helping Rachel to make clear the sequence and casual relationships within the story. She did this by asking Rachel questions; these serve as models so that on future occasions Rachel would be able to revise alone.

Writing to communicate

So far I have looked at writing which is school-based; the children were writing for themselves or for the teacher. Their concern was for the writing itself, for finding the most appropriate means of expressing what they wanted to say. The final example in this chapter is of writing with a specific audience in mind. Children need to have opportunities to use written language for genuine communication, and to see the effect that their writing can have on others.

As part of their Humanities work a Year 4 class had been looking at media reporting of the Gulf War of 1990/1; they had discussed how unbiased information could be obtained, and how one could take account of bias by comparing different accounts. A member of their teacher's family was serving as a soldier in the Gulf War and the children wrote to him asking for first-hand information. The soldier replied to them and when he returned home came to visit the class in school. This project gave the children many opportunities to think carefully about what they were reading and writing, and to consider how the way in which words are chosen and sentences structured can very subtly alter the received meaning. In writing for a specific, though unknown audience, the children had to be aware of possible interpretations of what they were writing, and to be sure that they were being explicit enough.

Figure 5.1 is an example of a letter written by Adam. Adam's teacher told me that he tried hard to find the right tone for a friendly letter to someone he does not know. He has been successful in a number of ways. He adopts a conversational style ('I bet you would like to be home though.') and achieves a balance between

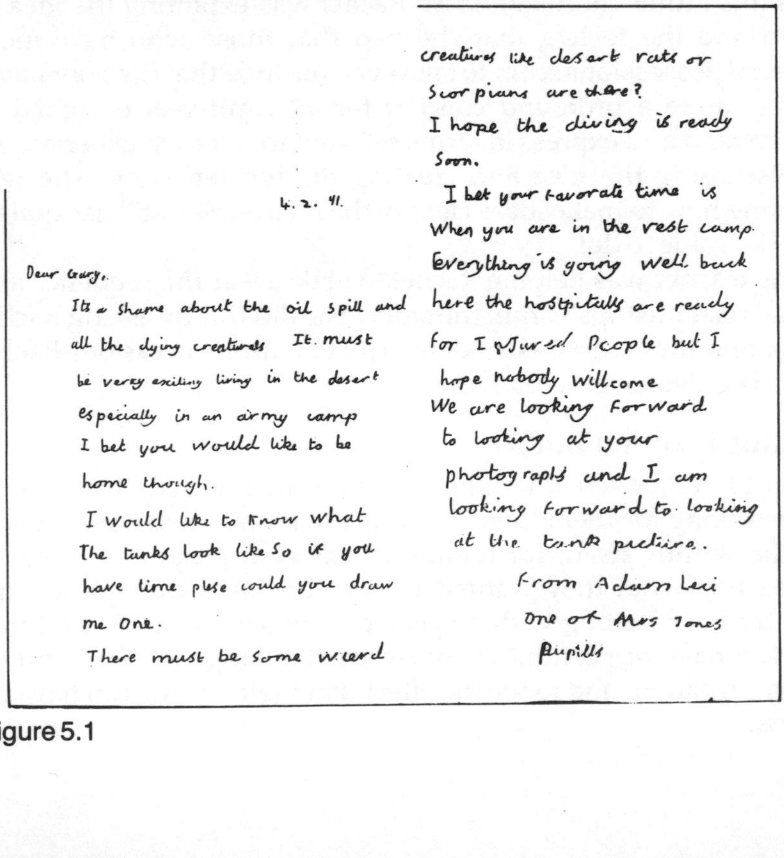

4. 2. 41.

Dear Gary,

It a shame about the oil spill and all the dying creatures It must be very exiting living in the desert especially in an army camp I bet you would like to be home though.

I would like to know what The tanks look like So if you have time plese could you draw me One.

There must be some weird creatures like desart rats or Scorpians are there?
I hope the diving is ready Soon.

I bet your favorate time is When you are in the rest camp. Everything is going well back here the hostpitales are ready for Injured People but I hope nobody willcome We are looking Forward to looking at your photographs and I am looking Forward to looking at the tanks picture.

From Adam Leci
One of Mrs Jones
Pupills

Figure 5.1

asking for information and passing on news; he asks for pictures of tanks, reminding Gary about this request at the end of the letter, and informs him about the preparation being done in hospitals. In places he has quite a sophisticated way of seeking for information without asking a direct question. The first sentence of the last paragraph is really a request for information if one reads between the lines. Note also how at the end of the letter he sums up all that he would like to receive from Gary!

Writing letters has always been a common activity in primary classrooms and yet so often they have been written in exercise books to be read only by a teacher with a red pen in her hand. Adam was engaged in genuine communication and he was able to evaluate his own success by the reply he received. This then enabled him to modify his own letter-writing style to match the reply. Unfortunately, I did not have access to these further letters but was informed of them by Adam's teacher. This project grasped the interest of the whole class: even the reluctant writers were keen to write when they saw others receiving replies from the Gulf. Children need to see that what they do in school is both rewarding in itself and relevant to life outside the classroom.

The use of word processors can also be a way of encouraging those children who find writing difficult or unappealing. The delight of writing with a word processor, as I myself can testify, is that one is liberated from the tyranny of poor handwriting. In writing this book, I have written a bit here and a bit there, I have been able to move paragraphs around, delete and insert sections of text and pick up where I left off without having to wade through the piles of paper which cover the floor of my study. I dread to think what it would have been like without my trusty word processor. Exactly the same principles apply to children's writing. They too must despair of writing when they are constantly making mistakes and the page gets grubbier and grubbier from excessive use of a rubber. The process of revision and editing becomes less attractive when it requires laborious re-writing by hand.

A teacher told me of working with a ten-year-old child who had been described as a 'reluctant writer'. His love for the computer meant that, although unwilling to write anything by hand, he would write stories on the computer. These stories revealed a quality which was not evident in the normal course of events. His teacher was looking with him at a story he had written and was now editing before printing it. The teacher was focussing on the

104

appropriate use of capital letters. The child was about to change the 'A' in BANG to lower case when he stopped and said to the teacher, 'No! I'm going to leave that word in capitals because then it looks loud.' My only regret is that I do not have a copy of the story. According to the teacher, the use of a word processing package freed that child to explore the writing process in a way which he would not have done otherwise.

The use of a word processor enables one to detach oneself from the physical act of writing and often gives one freedom to experiment. Writing on a screen seems less permanent than on paper or in an exercise book; frequently children seem more able to cope with the challenge of revising their work on the screen than on paper. They are more willing to 'have a go' and not so concerned with the final written product. The possibility of change is always there, but without the drudgery and grubbiness.

Concept keyboards are now frequently used in infant classrooms as a way of enabling children to write independently. It is, however, worth considering the nature of the writing which results and how this compares, for example, with the sort of writing which Sophie and Andy were producing, illustrated in chapter 4. The following example is by a five-year old girl in the reception class of a first school in a small town. The class had been doing some work on clowns and the teacher had created an overlay for the concept keyboard (fig.5.2). Hayley drew a picture of a clown (fig.5.4) and

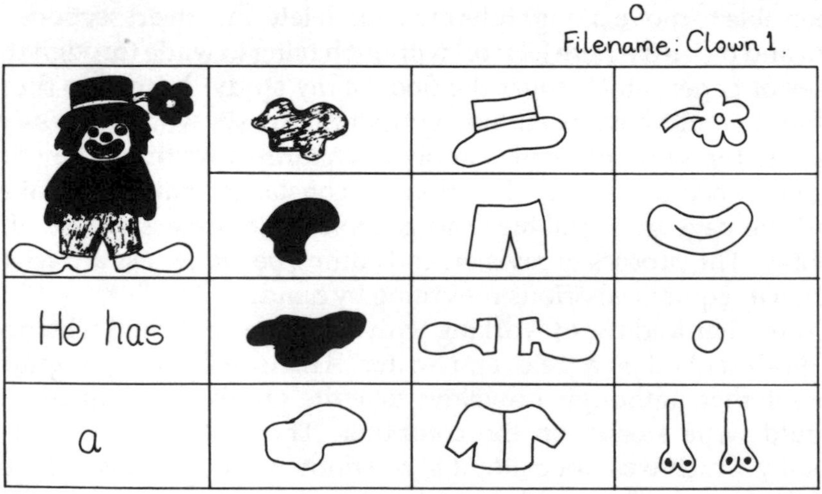

Figure 5.2

Here is a clown. He has a
blue hat. He has a
greenshirt. He has red
boots. He has yellow
trousers. He has a blue
flower. He has a yellow
nose.

Hayley

Figure 5.3

Figure 5.4

then used the concept keyboard to write a description of her clown (fig.5.3). Hayley succeeded in producing a quite long and full description of the clown, which, according to the teacher, gave her enormous pleasure and satisfaction. However, even though Hayley was making choices about her clown the choices were limited, constrained by the vocabulary available on the overlay. The sentence structure was also limited by the overlay and it could be said that Hayley's writing was merely following a pre-determined formula.

Desk-top publishing is another way of enhancing the reality of children's writing; they can now present their work in a way that is exciting and relates to printed materials that children will have seen at home. It is often used to produce class or school newspapers; children can be highly motivated and rewarded by seeing their work reproduced in such a way.

In considering children as they develop as readers and writers I have tried to answer the questions, 'Why do some children stop reading?' and 'Why do some children hate writing?' I have suggested that the answers to these questions surely lie in the sort of reading and writing that children are required to do in school, and the extent to which they are motivated and feel in control of their learning. In concluding this chapter, let us try to isolate some of the factors that have emerged from the case studies. I have identified three main points.

1. *Interest and motivation*

We have seen the importance of interest and motivation. Darren gave as his main reason for not reading the fact that the books he was given to read in school were boring. He was, therefore, not motivated to read and plodded slowly and painfully through the scheme without any enjoyment. It was only when he found books that he really enjoyed that he began to read with enthusiasm and involvement. The task for Darren's teacher now is to build on and develop his growing interest in books.

Often children come to school with a strong motivation to read and write. They may have learned at home that reading and writing are the most important skills they will learn at school and so they come eagerly awaiting this great event. Imagine their disappointment when faced with the dull books of the reading schemes published 20, 30 or 40 years ago. On a personal note, my husband is an avid reader in his professional life, but does not read at all for pleasure. He tells how he loved dogs and so was keen to find out all about Rover in his first book as a young child at school. His interest was aroused by the first page of the book, which stated that 'Kitty saw Rover', illustrated with a picture of a beautiful dog. He eagerly turned the page to find out more about this dog only to be told that 'Rover saw Kitty' and that was the end of that! I am sure that this tale has been embellished over the years but the essential point remains. Children are motivated to read and it is our responsibility to maintain and fuel that motivation. The child who is struggling with schoolwork is not likely to be motivated by the desire to please the teacher and succeed. In cases when we fail it is a human characteristic to denegrate that at which we are unsuccessful.

2. *Control*

We have seen that when children are given control of their own literacy behaviour, they feel less vulnerable and more likely to try new things. Darren, Kate and Rebecca — who were interviewed in chapter 2 — expressed their dislike of reading aloud to the teacher. They all felt embarrassment at the thought that their failings and inadequacies were being made public. When Darren was given the chance to choose his own book and to read it privately he began to enjoy reading. As children get older, the different abilities within a class can become more obvious, and the children become more sensitive about these differences. The notions of ownership and control are central in encouraging children's continued development as readers and writers, though they are, of course, important in the reception class as well.

3. *Relevance*

Children respond to reading and writing activities that they see as interesting in themselves and relevant to life outside school. Children who are given the freedom to practise and use their literacy skills in ways which are a natural part of their current interests and enthusiasms, are more likely to develop a wide variety of complex literacy behaviours.

It is clear that there is no one answer to the questions we have posed. For every child who loses interest in reading and writing there will be a mixture of different reasons. However, I do believe that we have identified some central principles that can assist us when finding a way forward for reluctant readers and writers. Two further concerns, however, are abundantly clear. Children continue to need teaching in literacy even when they are fluent readers and writers and we need to listen to their perceptions to discover the messages that we are teaching about literacy.

CHAPTER SIX
Reading and Writing for Learning

I begin this chapter with a consideration of classroom learning in general and in particular the role of literacy in the learning process, before going on to consider examples of children engaged in reading and writing for learning.

Classroom learning

In his description of 'real' learning, Rogers (1979) identifies some characteristics of the process. He notes that it necessitates personal involvement, is self-initiated, pervasive, evaluated by the learner and has its essence in meaning. The aim of education, Rogers says, is to facilitate such learning. Much classroom practice in the primary school is based on the idea of a young child as an active learner, forming and developing concepts through action on the environment. In primary classrooms, the provision of a stimulating environment is frequently seen as playing a major part in the facilitation of active learning; children are encouraged to explore, hypothesise and solve problems. The Piagetian view of learning through action is stressed in the Plowden Report (1967) where the child is described as the 'agent of his own learning'. This echoes passages in the Hadow Report (1931), arguing that '...the curriculum is to be thought of in terms of activity and experience, rather than of knowledge to be acquired and facts to be stored.' More recently Katz (1987) in an article which explores the nature of the curriculum for young children, says,

> Preschool and kindergarten programs should provide opportunities for interaction, active rather than passive activities, spontaneous play which can be provided for by setting up the environment ... and group projects that extend over time so that children can strengthen their disposition for sustained interest. (p.ii)

The emphasis on active learning can be traced back over at least 60 years; it would seem to be well established that what counts as learning in a primary classroom is not the accumulation of facts but the process of actively making sense of the world.

The notion of active developmental learning is strongly influenced by the ideas of Piaget, whose work on the development of cognition informs much thinking about early childhood education. He argues that children pass through various 'stages of development' and that each stage is characterised by the development of particular concepts and forms of thinking.

Donaldson (1978) criticises Piaget's methodology for failing to place the 'test questions' within a meaningful context for the child, leading to an underestimation of children's cognitive abilities. She coined the term 'embedded thinking' to describe thinking that is concerned with the immediate context and that satisfies immediate goals. Much of traditional child-centered pedadogy exploits this supposed limited nature of children's thinking; teachers are concerned to start 'where a child is', to ground activities in ways which are familiar to children and to select topics that are based on their recent personal experiences. Donaldson argues that this is not enough; children need to be helped to extend and develop their thinking beyond the immediate, that is, to engage in 'disembedded thought'. This view is supported by Tamburrini (1986) who says that schools should enable thinking to become increasingly 'disembedded'.

The notion that learning comes about through the physical and cognitive activity of the individual forces us to recognise the autonomy of the learner; the individual child becomes the focus of attention in the classroom. The implications of this for classroom management and organisation are considerable. Opportunities are provided for a variety of activities; the environment is constructed to facilitate problem-solving activities; individual work programmes are devised and the teacher needs to be aware of the developmental needs of each child.

Walkerdine (1983), however, criticises Piaget for failing to take into account the social construction of knowledge. She argues that a classroom is a social environment and learning cannot be considered only in terms of the individual. Pedagogy is inevitably bound up with views of learning. A purely developmental viewpoint results in a pedagogy of observation and individual development, with teacher intervention facilitating further development.

Walkerdine identifies a paradox in Piagetian theory: an emphasis on the individual in theory, results in practice in the normalisation of children and of the learning process. What counts as learning in a primary classroom is measured against some expectation of a series of developmental 'norms'.

The emergence of a constructivist approach in developmental psychology has reasserted the notion of 'the child as a social being' (Bruner and Haste 1987); this approach owes much to the work of Vygotsky (1978). He emphasises the dialectical relationship between the social and the individual. As Bruner says,

> the child's development depends upon her using, so to speak, the tool kit of the culture to express the powers of the mind. (p.5)

Thus the child learns the particular 'ways of thought' of the culture of which s/he is a part, first 'externally' in interaction with others, and then 'internally'; the social process is a precursor of the individual process. It would therefore be more appropriate to talk about 'learning stances or styles' rather than 'stages of development'.

A constructivist approach to learning would question the statement made earlier, on the basis of Piagetian thinking, that learning comes about through the activity of the individual learner, and would argue that alongside this must be placed consideration of a meaningful social context. Thus alongside the aspects of classroom organisation and management already mentioned must be placed opportunities for interaction and discussion; group problem-solving, discussion and investigations form an essential part of classroom life.

The role of the teacher in facilitating learning has been foremost in other considerations of learning and pedagogy. Bruner (1968) describes that learning as the construction and employment of strategies to resolve the problems that learners encounter in their lives. This takes place through action, sensory organisation and the use of language. Eisner (1982) extends Bruner's description and argues against separating the affective and the cognitive. Both Bruner and Eisner see the teacher as playing an active role in helping children to encode their experiences. Katz (1987) maintains that children need help to make sense of their environment if they are not to 'starve in the midst of plenty' (p 87). Donaldson (1978) argues that teachers must help children consciously to direct their own thinking and to reflect on their actions, physical and mental.

The current debate on literacy learning can profitably be considered in terms of the distinction raised earlier in this chapter between embedded and disembedded thought, and in terms of children as active learners. The approaches that stress 'meaning' (Goodman 1976, Smith 1978) see reading as essentially a sense-making process, in which children bring meanings to a text and take meanings from it through their active engagement. Work on early writing (Clay 1979) also stresses children's active involvement, as their mark-making is gradually recognised as transmission of meaning. Literacy learning is seen as a continuation of oral language learning; children make sense of the language they continually see and hear around them, responding as readers and writers, continually refining their behaviours in the light of new experiences.

I shall now hold these ideas up against practical classroom activities, and look at children using literacy skills in learning across the curriculum.

Learning in the classroom

The rest of this chapter is devoted to describing the work of one teacher, Teresa. She is the Upper School Curriculum Co-ordinator in a large primary school, responsible for

encouraging teachers within Years 3,4,5,6 to deliver the curriculum in a manner acceptable to themselves as professionals, to the pupils' needs, encompassing statutory requirements, which at the same time would not curtail their individual initiatives, cramp their teaching styles, and impose conformity and control just for the sake of complying to Government recommendations.

(This is how Teresa described her role in the introduction to an M.A. thesis she wrote about her teaching.)

The school has 450 pupils on roll and is situated in the inner area of an industrial city. 80% of the pupils are of Asian origin, 10% Afro-Caribbean and 10% white Caucasian. The majority of pupils use English as their second language. Over half the pupils in the school are on the special needs register, with problems including school phobia, learning difficulties, emotional problems and a history of child abuse. In the area surrounding the school housing conditions are poor and unemployment is widespread. There is a strong working relationship between parents and staff;

counselling, help with form filling and advice on financial matters are available, and parents are made to feel welcome inside the school. Saturday morning art clubs are organised for the pupils and many activities for parents take place in the Parents' Room, in order to encourage links with the staff. The environment of the school reflects the multilingual abilities of its pupils and their parents, with all notices and displays in several languages.

Teresa began to reconsider her approach to teaching as her concern grew that both she and the other teachers in the Upper School were encountering difficulties in implementing the National Curriculum in a purposeful and meaningful manner. Their concerns were echoed by a discussion paper on curriculum organisation and practice by Alexander, Rose and Woodhead (1991) which said,

> H.M.I. inspections over the last two years show that standards in Key Stage 1 are generally better than in Key Stage 2. This is the result of a better match of work to ability in Key Stage 1 than in Key Stage 2 particularly for the more able pupils and adds force to the view that many class teachers especially in Year 5 and 6 have difficulty covering the whole curriculum in sufficient depth. (p.15)

I shall begin by outlining Teresa's approach, as she told it to me, and go on to describe some work done in the classroom and some examples of the children's writing and reading.

The main thesis behind this classroom approach to literacy is that unless the emotions are affected, the pupils' writing will not be truly creative or imaginative. The teacher's aim is for the children to realise there is no such thing, in this context, as a right or wrong answer. Through drama and role play she aims to 'empower' the children, so that they can make meaning of their classroom activities. The phrase 'make meaning' is central to Teresa's philosophy. The variety of cultural and religious backgrounds within the class means that a whole range of understandings are brought to the experiences created. In making meaning the children are synthesising their own and each other's interpretations; in the move from the particular to the universal, ideas and concepts are understood because they have been felt. Teresa said, 'In order to write you must feel, otherwise why do you need to keep a record of it?' Creative writing must come from an affective experience which is real and which leads to a genuine desire to write about it. Learning takes place when the affective is fused with the cognitive. Drama is the context for Teresa's provision for meaning making, because pupils are here engaged both affectively and cognitively; they want to learn more because there is a specific reason for learning.

Teresa was greatly influenced by the work of Dorothy Heathcote who came to the school to work with her class for a few sessions. I shall describe that work and how it acted as a starting point for a further ten months of classroom activities.

The Mary Morgan project

This project was done with a class of 30 Year 4 pupils. Most of the children were bilingual and one was just beginning to speak English at school. Eight pupils were on the special needs register and six were described by the teacher as 'non-readers'. The drama sessions took place on three separate mornings but other work stemming from this lasted for ten months.

Mary Morgan was a young servant of a family living in Maesllwch Castle in the early 1800s. It was well known that the squire's son had taken a strong liking to the 15-year-old girl and there was a cover-up campaign to divert scandal when Mary became pregnant. However, evidence seems to suggest that the child was the result of rape by the squire himself, although the son openly declared himself to be the father. Seconds after she had given birth Mary used an expensive penknife to murder her child. Mary lies buried in unconsecrated ground, her resting place marked by two stones. One was paid for by a friend of the judge who had ordered her hanging.

Teresa describes her reaction to the project:

My teaching had been focussed on the coverage of attainment targets and teaching of skills. I was becoming a quantitative teacher rather than a qualitative teacher, relying on ready-manufactured commercial schemes and deluding myself by thinking that as I ploughed through the statutory requirements of National Curriculum I was in fact an efficient teacher.

My choice of banal topics such as transport, weather or clothes strengthens my claim as to how boring and predictable I had become. In that particular frame of mind I would never have chosen the Mary Morgan story as a context for teaching and learning. Rape, murder, suffering, hanging were not within my pupils' experience, and furthermore, I would not have mentioned anything about burials or funerals due to the various religious doctrines operant in my classroom. My own ignorance of my pupils' rites, rituals and religious ceremonies would have prevented me from even sharing my own experiences of this taboo subject.

Up until now I had shielded my pupils from the very thing I had wanted them to become aware of, and that is knowledge of being totally human and relating to each other accordingly, regardless of colour, class or creed. Because of my own fear of dealing with controversial topics such as death, murder and the complexity of human relations I had chosen to play safe; after all the children were only eight years old and what could they possibly know about life at that age? How wrong I was to be. For years I had protected my pupils from the very thing they were experiencing in their everyday life – human relationships.

The project was presented in several dramatic episodes. I shall describe all of these but only go into the details of those which are most pertinent to the subject matter of this book.

Discussion

The work began with a discussion on what was involved in being a detective. The children came up with ideas which were written on the board by the teacher. These were:
- needing a magnifying glass
- spying on someone
- looking at a map
- you have to be good at working together
- taking photographs
- keeping on being clever
- always using our brain

During this discussion the children had identified for themselves many of the skills which form an essential part of the National Curriculum, such as observation, map reading, fine discrimination, co-operation, tolerance, empathy, visual discrimination, classification, listening and problem solving.

The children were then asked if they were willing to carry on as detectives in order to solve a mystery. They agreed and the project continued. I am not sure what would have happened if they had not agreed!

Reading the gravestones

The children were shown copies of the two gravestones of Mary Morgan. The inscription read,

To the memory of Mary Morgan who young and beautiful, endowed with a good understanding and disposition but unenlightened by the sacred truths of Christianity, became the victim of sin and shame and was condemned to an ignominious death on the 11th April 1805 for the murder of her bastard child. Roused to a first sense of guilt and remorse by the eloquent and humane exertions of her benevolent judge Mr Justice Hardinge, she underwent the sentence of the law on the following Thursday with unfeigned repentance and a fervent hope of forgiveness through the merits of a redeeming intercessor. This stone is erected not merely to perpetuate the remembrance of a departed penitent but to remind the living of the frailty of human nature when unsupported by religion.

The language was extremely difficult but the children were encouraged to work together, looking at the inscription as a whole rather than attempting to decipher individual words, in order to try and 'make meaning'. Because their imaginations had been captured the children were highly motivated; because they were highly motivated they were successful. The reading activity was embedded in a context which provided the children with the support they needed.

At different levels the children came to understand that print conveys meaning. The non-readers were able to distinguish between letters and numbers and to appreciate more the functional nature of print and the value of being able to read for information. The more experienced readers came to understand that the messages which print conveys are open to different interpretations.

Making a map

The children were then asked to make a map of the local town, Presteigne, in order to create the environment of the story. They were given the materials required, including cards on which were written the street names. In this activity the children were engaged in symbolic representation, again embedded in a context which enabled them to operate at a much higher level than in more traditional disembedded school tasks. Again they were reading and classifying and using print materials for a variety of purposes.

Creating the community

The children were given cards which put them into role as members of the town. They were required to place their homes or different settings on the map and so had to discuss and negotiate with each other.

He was kind and person he looked after his children and his wife he had 2 boys and 1 girl he died in a car accident while during in a car his relatis and famly were sad he died in 1805 his hobblies were reading football and writing and running in the morning.

David Wilkins
Religon. Welsh.
. mudered Jhone walks
and David got hung
—oved husband of
Mary Bonds Wilkins
his wife was pregnant
t when she hard she
got mad and misscarried
r baby.

---

harles was a very
nice man. He loved
ds, he was 19
ears old his fou-
rite popstar was
arlie Minouge His
mother was German
so Charles was
recost. He is know
berried at Saint
Maithues Church.

Jenny Corkins
Age 7.
died from aids.
Mothers name
Lise. Fathers
name Jhon.
Born 1693 best
friend's name
Katy Richards
Age 8.
Died in 1805.
Her dreams
was to be a
air hostess.
Her grave is
in prestaigru.

Designing our
graveyard.

In the
memory
of Roland
mains age 60
died in 27 December
1706 died from
cancer he had 3
chidren and a wife He
loved fish and chips

Charles Morgan
died of cancer
was Engaged to
Mary Jorsa He
died in 1805
Charles Morgan
was beloved son
of Tasleem Morgan
and Josh Morgan
had no brothers
or sisters

Figure 6.1

Creating the graveyard

The children then wrote gravestones which were placed in the graveyard of the church, creating the past of the community. Figure 6.1 shows examples of the children's writing.

Examination of the writing on these 'gravestones' shows a variety of ideas about what is appropriate content. Some are close to convention, for example those of Charles Morgan and Roland Mains. Others are written in continuous prose and tell a mini-story. The epitaphs are also revealing of the children's understanding of time; one talks of someone killed in a car accident in 1805 and another who died of Aids in the same year; an illustration perhaps of how bound up these children are in the here and now. Other children have an acute understanding of the effects of tragedy as in the child who writes about the wife who miscarried when she heard of her husband's death. It is also interesting to see how nationality and religion are linked in the children's minds; one character's religion is described as Welsh. Teresa identified this as an area needing further work in the classroom.

The arrival of the new vicar and his visit to the town

An adult in the role of the new vicar was shown round the town by the children, in their roles. They re-read the epitaphs to Mary Morgan and tried to make further sense of them. Teresa writes of this,

It could be argued that the reading content on the Mary Morgan graves-tones was above the pupils' actual intellectual capabilities... The pupils were encouraged to negotiate and define their own way of learning and to see that the stimulus, in this case the gravestones, could be understood by them in a variety of different ways. There was no one right answer. Drama enhanced the English National Curriculum by providing the pupils with an opportunity to make meaning from a text which had become personalised for them by the fact that they had been in role.

Meeting the archivists

The children were grouped for the purpose of finding more information about Mary Morgan. They organised themselves into groups of eight or nine, ensuring that in each group there was a fluent reader and an efficient scribe. The materials used were very adult compared with the commercially-produced scheme books to which the children were accustomed. However, even the poorest reader struggled to make meaning; in a normal classroom situation, when asked to come and read from his graded reader to the teacher, this same child would frequently not even attempt to decode let alone to make meaning. The activity of solving the mystery was embedded in a meaningful context and the skills required were those of a real life situation. As Teresa says, 'Making meaning and finding coherence from a jumbled assortment of facts was far more demanding than answering questions about a neatly organised text. The sharing of information from one group to another demanded precise choice of language, acute listening skills and avoidance of repetition... Knowledge ... was not being accrued in a linear fashion but it was being cross-referenced, reorganised, tested and shared with the group.'

Meeting the people – a living tableau

A group of drama students were in role, during one session, as people known by Mary Morgan. The children formulated appropriate questions to pose; they soon learned that the way in which a question was phrased affected the answer received. So revision of work was put into an immediate and relevant context. An example of these questions is given in figure 6.2.

Ceremony to honour Mary Morgan's grave

As part of this ceremony the children wrote tributes and poems. Some of these are reproduced in figures 6.3 and 6.4.

The haiku poems show an admirable strength of emotion within the discipline of a stipulated form. In writing these it would seem that the children have thought and discussed and felt the essence of the story. It is interesting to note that one of these poems was a collaborative attempt by Shirjeet and Sandeep; one can only speculate on the talk and revision process in which they must have engaged. Whatever, such an exercise created the opportunity for talking about language.

The tributes in Figure 6.3 show how the drama helped the children to write in role, from the point of view of an inhabitant of the town. This is unlikely to be achieved so effectively without the prior experiences which enabled the children to become people living in that small Welsh town during the scandal.

Putting the Cook in the hot Seat.
What did she feel Killing the baby?
does She eat know after Killing?
How do you feel at the moments?
How long have you Mary Morgan?
Do you ever try to speak to her ?
What did She do when She was Small.
                    Qestion Mary Morgan
Have you got a mother and father ?

Putting Mary morgan in the hot seat
What do you feel like ?
Have you been sad after you killed the baby?
Have you got friends?
What do you like doing?
When did you first start working for the wilkins?
Has Jhon wilkins met you after you killed the
baby?
Has the doctor seen you ?
How many times have you fell after killing the
baby?

Figure 6.2

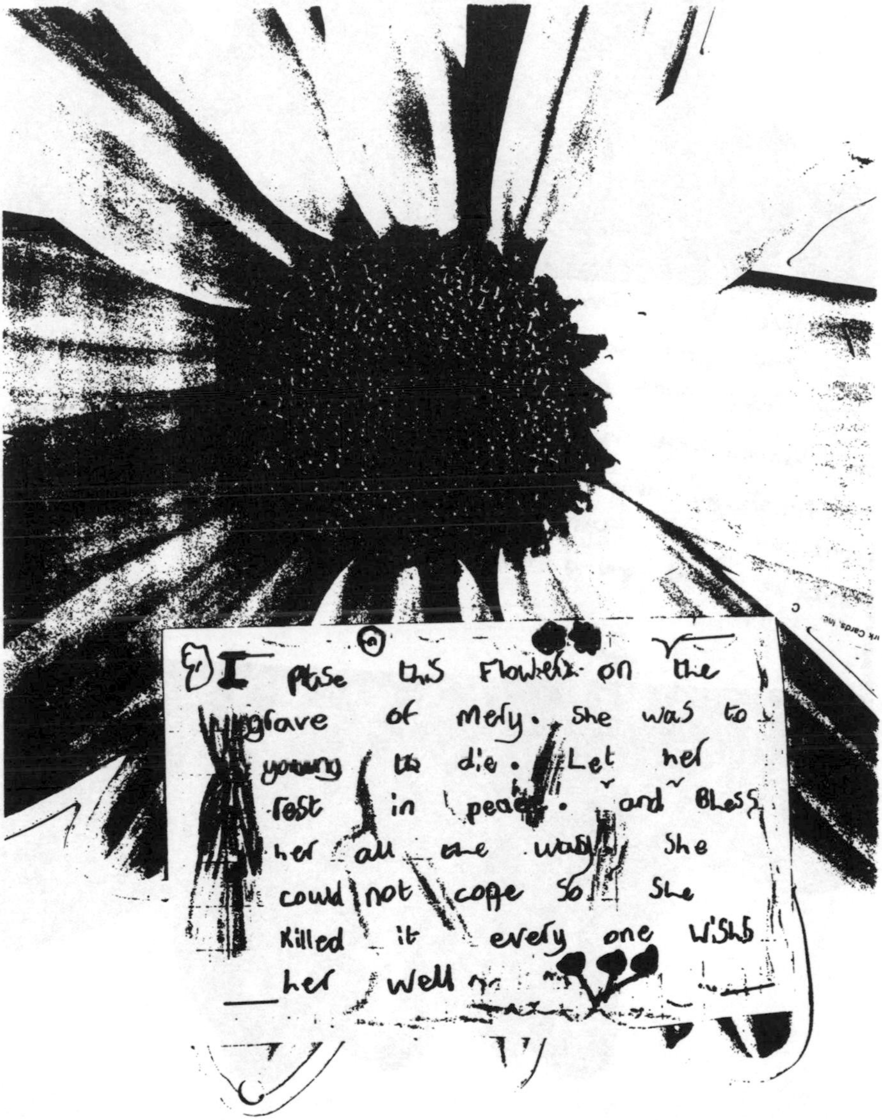
I plase this Flower on the
grave of mery. She was to
young to die. Let her
rest in peace. and Bless
her all the way. She
could not cope so she
killed it every one wishs
her well

Figure 6.3A

122

I place this flower on the grave of Mary Mongan.
Let your poor soul rest in peace now you have
your new home. And we all wish you a nice time
in heaven. We remember you. still in the little town
of Presteigne and we will remember you for years to
come. We still regret loosing you and you infant
child. We wish you a happy time in heaven.

Figure 6.3B

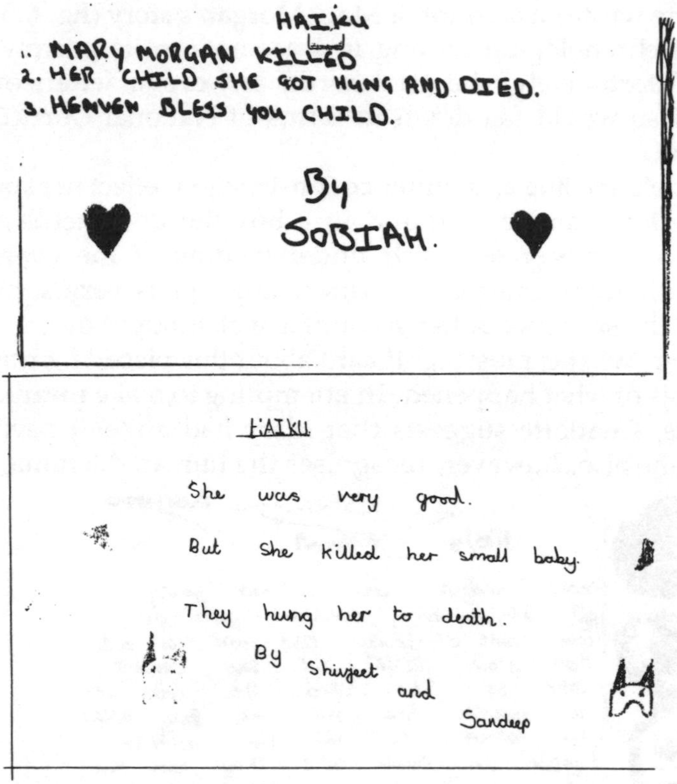

HAIKU

1. MARY MORGAN KILLED
2. HER CHILD SHE GOT HUNG AND DIED.
3. HEAVEN BLESS YOU CHILD.

By
SOBIAH.

HAIKU

She was very good.

But she killed her small baby.

They hung her to death.

By Shivjeet
and
Sandeep

Figure 6.4A

HAIKU

She is kind and nice

! She is sweet and soft sad and quiet

, Blue and white goodbye

By TRACEY

Figure 6.4B

Charlotte wrote an account of Mary Morgan's story (fig. 6.5). As a piece of chronological writing it is accurate in its portrayal of events. Unfortunately, she used hardly any capital letters or full stops and so would fall down in terms of National Curriculum assessment.

Charlotte's spelling and sentence construction reflect her spoken language, for example '…found in a box the documents', and 'dicidid'. In the way in which understanding of the events is reflected, though. Charlotte's written language is very sophisticated and the structure of her account is well thought out.

However, what is most significant about this piece of writing is the analysis of what happened. In attempting to make meaning of the events, Charlotte suggests that Mary had an 'evil devil' inside her; she also, however, recognises the human dilemma, 'she

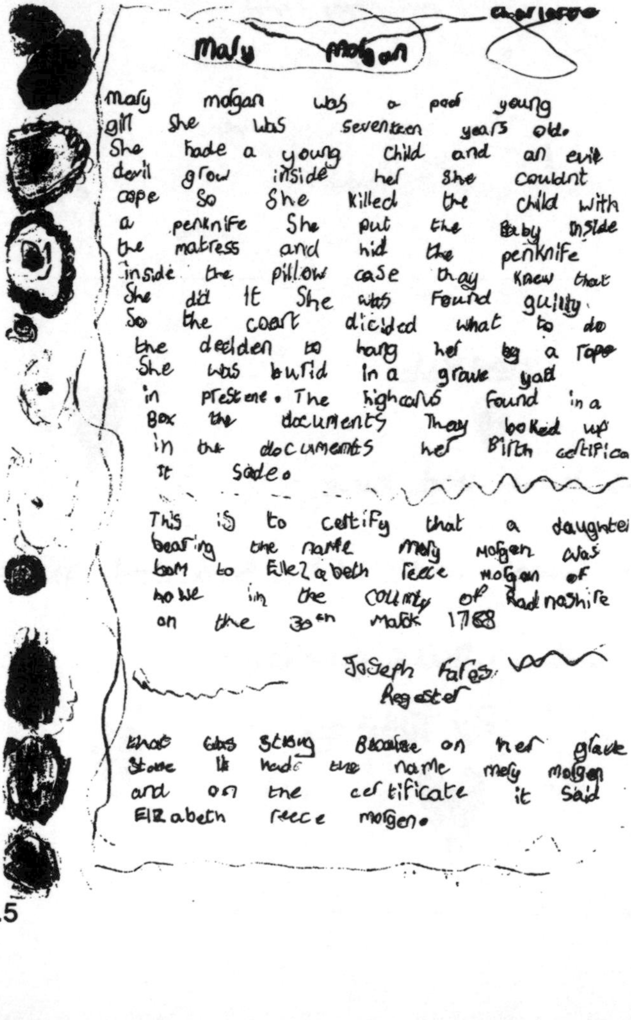
Charlotte

Maly Mogan

mary mogan was a poor young girl she was seventeen years old. She hade a young child and an evil devil grow inside her she couldnt cope So She killed the child with a penknife She put the baby inside the matress and hid the penknife inside the pillow case thay knew that She did It She was Found guilty. So the coart dicided what to do the decided to hang her by a rope She was burid in a grave yad in prestene. The highcarts found in a Box the documents They looked up in the documents her Birth certifica it sade.

This is to certify that a daughter bearing the name mary mogen was born to Elezabeth reece mogan of house in the county of Radnashire on the 30th march 1768

Joseph Fares
Regester

that was strong Because on her grave Stone it hade the name mery mogen and on the certificate it said Elizabeth reece mogen.

Figure 6.5

couldn't cope', and includes that in her explanation. Her description of the difference of name between the gravestone and the birth certificate shows an ability to reconcile inconsistencies.

The drama project certainly opened up opportunities for a wide range of literacy learning; because the activities were embedded in a context in which the children were totally involved, the children were able to attain literacy understandings at a level far higher than they had previously achieved in disembedded tasks. This can be referred back to Rogers' idea of 'real learning' described at the very start of this chapter. He wrote of the young child as an active learner, forming and developing concepts through action on the environment. In this situation the children were not only acting on the environment but creating the environment themselves; in so doing they were also constructing a literacy which operated within that context and empowered them to act as literate people.

Torn in two

The second example of work done in this class is on the theme: *Why do people behave strangely when they are under pressure?* I will describe this in less detail than the Mary Morgan project and concentrate on giving examples of the children's writing. The final product of this project was an opera entitled *Torn in two* and all the examples of writing come from the script of this. The focus of my analysis will, therefore, be the 'authorship' rather than the 'secretarial' skills.

The starting point of the project was the teacher asking the class to think of three things that made them happy and three things that made them sad. Their responses to this led to discussions about feeling under pressure. The class then created collaboratively the story which became the plot of the opera. It tells of a little girl whose father died and who works out her grief by becoming a bully at school. This led the children into the need for looking beneath the surface and searching for the hidden motives for behaviour. They were making meaning of the story and learning that everybody, even the apparently unsympathetic person, has a story to tell.

Extracts from the script are given below; as in all operas there is some dialogue and some songs. The writing was done collaboratively but unfortunately I have no record of this process, only the final product.

Amelia: I feel so alone. I've lost so much. Life is so hard for me since Dad died. I had to take all the responsibility. I wish there was someone I could talk to, but he was the only one who listened. Mum tries but it's not the same she doesn't understand the way he did. He always asked me to take care of her when he wasn't here. The kids at school have such a good life, they have a mum and dad, people they can rely on. All they have to do is think about school and what they are going to wear at parties. Why did it have to be me? They are all so happy, I can't stand to see people so happy when I'm so miserable inside.

This is the opening speech of the opera and it is interesting that the children have chosen to begin by revealing the heart of the bully, thus creating sympathy for her with the audience. I consider it a very powerful piece of writing in the way in which it empathises with the feelings of Amelia as she tries to come to terms with the death of her father. There is the mixture of self pity, reason and resentment which is so common in such circumstances. There is no hint that Amelia is the bully, except in the final sentence; this is a very clever way of preparing for what is to come.

This piece of dialogue comes when some children are playing in the playground.

Sukhvinder: Get lost!

Amelia: You shut up. You are only a stupid idiot. (*starts to spoil the game*) Stop playing or I'll hit you. Do you want a fight?

Terry: Stop it you big bully.

Julie: Leave us alone.

Baljit: Why don't you go and fight someone else?

Amelia: Who is going to make me? Are you going to make me move from here?

Children play hopskotch. Amelia kicks the stone away.

Amelia: Only babies play this. Go and fetch your stone.

Children: Stop pestering us go and play your own game. Why are you doing this to us?

Amelia: Shut up you are not my father. You are all soft sissies.

Amelia sees Royston and goes over.

Amelia: What are you staring at you goggled gook?

Royston: Stop it or I'll tell the teacher.

Amelia: I ain't scared of the teacher they can't smack you anyway.

Royston: What's your problem dood?

Amelia: What's it to you?

Song:	*(Amelia and Royston sing alternate verses.)*
	Why do you stand there just watching?
	Who do you think you are?
	I've not seen you in my playground,
	Just where have you come from?
	Why are you being so cruel?
	Why do you spoil all their games?
	Why should you ask all the questions?
	I won't tell you who I am.

This scene follows on immediately from the opening speech and Amelia's public behaviour contrasts with the private sorrow we saw earlier. The writers have conveyed this by their use of language; the sentences are shorter and disconnected from each other, the words are more colloquial and Amelia's frequent questioning reflects the aggressive challenge she is throwing at the other children.

Royston seems to represent someone from outside the crowd who is not impressed by the bully and is prepared to stand up to her. It is interesting to note that the use of slang words increases in this confrontation. The writers seem to recognise that use of language and choice of words can convey the nature of an interaction. The questions of the first two stanzas of the song also reflect this confrontation.

The writers establish cohesion very well throughout the script. I highlighted the remark at the end of the opening speech where Amelia reveals her resentment of the other children and in this section her remark, 'You are not my father', reminds us of the hurt she is feeling inside. This is a sophisticated technique used well.

The next scene is in the classroom.

Voiceover:	Those who haven't finished their work will be staying in at lunchtime. Everyone's work is so untidy, you forget your margins, you forget the date, your work is disgusting, you forget your full stops, your handwriting is untidy. Where do capital letters go?
Children:	At the beginning of a sentence.
Voiceover:	And what about the title? You underline with a ruler. Your pencils are not sharpened. Fourth years who can't even write properly. Well you wait till you get to secondary school they won't stand for any nonsense. *(paper flicking)*

128

> Who keeps flicking that paper? Who wants their hands
> chopping off? I'm not sitting in this dustbin with you lot. So
> clean it up right now. Royston get yourself off to the
> headmaster's office and tell him that you are a litter bug.

This part is a wonderful insight into the children's perceptions of what it means to be a teacher and what is involved in the writing process. Note how the concern is with presentation qualities although this is something which is not given first priority in this classroom. The teacher's role is portrayed as one of primarily keeping control through very negative statements; this is very different from how the children's teacher came across to me but such is the power of convention. Again the children's use of language and sentence structure convey the feeling behind what they are saying. The repetition of a short question form builds up the picture of an angry teacher. Perhaps the children here are truly writing from experience.

The next scene takes place in Amelia's mother's bedroom where there is a large photograph of the father; she sings this song which has a repeating refrain:

> Life was so much different then
> When we had him around,
> He was there to comfort us
> We had everything.

Refrain:
> He made us happy
> He made us glad,
> We had such fun
> Never sad.

> He came home after work,
> We were a family,
> But now there's something missing
> We've lost everything.

Refrain.

> What are we going to do now,
> How can we forget
> All the pain and guilt we feel
> He was everything.

Refrain.

Amelia: Don't worry I'm here I'll look after you.

I find it interesting that this song and indeed the whole opera reflects a very conventional picture of family life although this is not the experience of a large number of the children. The father is seen as the strong one, going out to work, supporting the family, while the mother and daughter are completely dependent on him. Amelia's feeling that she has to take over the support of her mother is the partial cause of her tremendous stress.

Again the ability of the children to empathise with the feelings of a person who has lost someone important is impressive; they identify the mixture of pain and guilt and the contrast between the fullness of life then and its emptiness now.

The mother receives a phone call from the school informing her of Amelia's bullying. She tells Amelia that it must stop but Amelia refuses to discuss it. Amelia then sings this song:

Something makes me do it
Something deep inside
I can't let them see me suffering
My feelings I must hide.
> Anger, loss, confusion,
> Emptiness, tears and pain.
Why should they be so happy
They don't know what I've lost.
They must never know my feelings
No matter what the cost.
> Anger, loss, confusion
> Emptiness, tears and pain.
I've got to take his place
She needs me to be strong
I've got to fix things for her
When everything goes wrong.
> Anger, loss, confusion,
> Emptiness, tears and pain.

The power of emotion in this song is striking. The writers have really come to grips with Amelia's inner anguish and you can see how they are looking beneath the outward behaviour and finding an explanation. They have succeeded in conveying a set of very complex emotions. The simple structure of the song is effective; the rhyme and rhythm and repeating refrain builds up tension and emotion.

The scene then moves to Royston's home, a traditional happy household where Royston and his family sit and discuss Amelia.

Royston sees that Amelia has problems and appreciates his own comfortable life. Later in school Amelia and Royston are in an art lesson; they are painting a picture of flowers and Amelia spoils Royston's picture. They then sing alternate verses of this song:

Flowers don't last for ever
They only wilt and die
Their beauty is for a moment
When its gone it makes you cry

Why have you spoilt my painting
You're such a mixed up creep
I fail to understand you
Does anything make you weep

What do you know about crying
What do you know about pain
Drawing pretty pictures
Life is not a game

What are you trying to tell me
Is there something you want to say
I promise to stop and listen
I won't go out to play.

Go out to play don't listen
You wouldn't understand
I don't need help from anyone
Go hold your Daddy's hand.

The children have again succeeded in conveying the tensions and mixed up emotions. The hints and allusions throughout and the gradual coming to understanding is counterbalanced with Amelia's continuing aggression. Some lines could be dismissed as cliches, for example 'Life is not a game' but the power of other lines, for example the parallels implied in the first stanza, well compensate.

The play ends with Amelia sharing her problem with Royston.

Royston: Are you trying to say something?
Amelia: No, I can't tell this to anyone. It's for me to know and me to sort out.
Royston: Come on. I know you've got something to tell me. Perhaps I can help.

Amelia: I want to tell you but it is just so painful I don't know how.

Royston: Just tell me. I can keep a secret.

Amelia: I wish he was here.

Royston: You wish who was here?

Amelia: My dad.

Royston: Why where is he?

Amelia: He got killed in the line of duty trying to stop a fight

Royston: I'm really sorry. I don't know what I'd do if my dad died.

Amelia: I always used to talk to my dad. He was my best friend.

Royston: Well maybe we can all be friends now. I know we can't replace your dad but now we know what's wrong we'll try to help.

Amelia: When you've lost someone you care for,
(song) You don't know what to do.
Inside you scream and shout,
But do not let it out.
You take it out on those who care,
You don't realise till they're not there
Why do I have to be me
Inside I'm so lonely.

The play ends, not with a neat and tidy resolution of everything but an indication that there is hope and things will begin to get better. I feel this is quite a mature understanding of the situation; the recognition that Amelia is still hurting inside but that she herself is now coming to terms with it and that the process of talking about something is the start of healing. In this the children are identifying their own learning process. Through drama and role play they enter into a situation and so their writing is given an immediacy which it would be difficult to achieve otherwise.

In writing the opera they have been writing for a real purpose and a genuine audience. They have written in a variety of forms: dialogue and poetry in the opera itself, and notes, continuous prose and diagrams in the preparation process. They have written in different voices, adopting appropriate language for roles and situations. They have written collaboratively and so made explicit the writing process through which we all go; they have drafted, edited and revised. They needed to do this because the opera was going to be performed and they had to arrive at a final script. This was a case of 'real' writing.

Conclusion

These descriptions of children's reading and writing show how the quality of literacy behaviours can be raised when children start from their own first-hand experiences. Teresa used drama as her way of enabling the children to enter into the emotions surrounding particular events. Because the children had felt and experienced emotions when they were in role, their writing was alive and powerful; because they had to make sense of a text in order to proceed with an enquiry they worked hard at it to understand what it was they needed to know. These two projects, show how the children were able to tune into emotions and dilemmas at a very adult and demanding level. Teresa used the breadth of experiences and cultural understandings in her classroom as an advantage in this respect. The children had to take into account each other's point of view in coming to their own meaning. Teresa says that she uses affective learning as the way into cognitive learning and this certainly seems to be reflected in these projects. Each led on into a wide range of activites covering all areas of the curriculum. The classroom became the Welsh town of Presteigne during that time and it became a school with a hurting bully during that project. What is most important is the fact that the children were totally involved in and immersed in what they were doing; they were engaged in 'real' learning for their own purposes, not just to fulfil the requirements of an imposed curriculum.

It seems appropriate to close with a letter written by a child in Teresa's Year 6 class to Kenneth Clarke, the then Secretary of State for Education (fig. 6.6). The class wanted to do more drama but Teresa had explained to them about the National Curriculum requirements and assessments and how that constrained what they did in the classroom. Sukdip decided to put her case to the Secretary of State; I do not know what the response was! This is the first rough draft before it was edited for spelling and punctuation, but here is writing which is genuine communication, expressing strongly held views in a cogently argued form and wanting a response.

Dear   Mr clark.

I am writing this letter to show what my opinions are. I do not think maths and ~~sice~~ since and other subjects are not really important the most important thing is what happens around us what happens in the real world. I do agree that we have to learn these subjects to help us in life but they very important they are only important to help us in life the real thing that is important we learn ~~or~~ what is going to happen to us when we grow up what kind of experenc we might ~~we~~. get in the real world we should learn how to protect our selves in the real world.

your sincerley

Sukdip Johal age 10.

P.S. think about what I have written

Figure 6.6

CHAPTER SEVEN

Literacy Beyond Teachers

The emphasis throughout this book has been on the social and cultural definitions of literacy that are created within classrooms. I have discussed how young children come to school with substantial experience of literacy behaviours and some understandings of the ways in which they have seen and heard reading and writing used by the significant others around them. Think back to the example of Donna, which was given in chapter 2; remember how she showed some real literacy understanding which was not recognised by her teacher. The problem was that the way in which Donna applied her developing literacy did not match the expectations of the school. The work of Shirley Brice Heath has been frequently quoted in this book, further illustrating the fact that school literacy and the literacy of the home are not always the same.

In this chapter I shall look at the way in which parents help their children to become readers and writers. I shall examine what they actually do and how they know what to do. I shall go on to look at the roles parents play in schools, and how the literacies created in the home can work together in the classroom with the literacy of the school.

I begin by looking at a father reading to his son. Robert was nearly four and his father was reading his regular bedtime story to him. He was reading from *The House at Pooh Corner* by A. A. Milne, a favourite of the father's. There follows a transcript of the conversations that took place during the reading. For the sake of space I have not transcribed the text of the book, (chapter eight).

1 **Father:** Right. This is me reading Robert a story for the benefit of Margaret, isn't it.

2 **Robert:** No.

3 **F:** 'Tis. Margaret's listening too. All right? Happy now?

4 **R:** Yes Dad.

5 **F:**	Which book are we reading from? What's it called? Who's this?
6 **R:**	Pooh.
7 **F:**	Winnie the Pooh. The House at Pooh Corner.
8 **R:**	Yea.
9 **F:**	And we're reading chapter 8 'In which Piglet does a very grand thing.'
10 **R:**	Here's a book that I was reading.
11 **F:**	Yea. Now are you listening?
12 **R:**	Yea.
13 **F:**	Right now.

(Reads to the sentence '...when he had gone in and out once or twice just to make sure that he could get out again.')

14 **F:**	Do you remember once he got stuck in Rabbit's hole?
15 **R:**	Yea.
16 **F:**	Do you reckon that's what he means?
17 **R:**	Yea.

(a few minutes later)

18 **R:**	I want a drink.
19 **F:**	You want a drink? Well, let's finish the story first. Where did we get to? They were knocking at Owl's door weren't they?

(Later the father encourages Robert to join in reading with him.)

20 **F:**	'In a corner of the room' – look at the picture, there, see – 'the table-cloth began to
21 **R:**	move.
22 **F:**	'wriggle'. Do you know what it was?
23 **R:**	Piglet.

(A few lines on the father makes a mistake and corrects himself.)

24 **F:**	Owl, do you do that? He didn't say that at all, he said, 'Owl did you do that?'

(At the end of the chapter the father asks Robert about the story.)

25 **F:**	Was that a good story? So what happened to Owl's house?
26 **R:**	It blew over.
27 **F:**	It did, didn't it. How did they get out?
28 **R:**	Through the letter box.
29 **F:**	That's right. Who got out through the letter box?
30 **R:**	Piglet.

31 **F:**	That's right. Now was that a good story?
32 **R:**	Yea.
33 **F:**	Good, well it's bedtime now isn't it.
34 **R:**	No it's not.
35 **F:**	It is rascal. Right, turn the tape-off. Find the off switch.

What was happening during this story time? What was Robert learning about literacy? How did his father 'teach' him?

The question and answer session at the end of the story could almost have been between a teacher in school and a pupil. Robert's father adopts a very teacherly tone, and asks a succession of closed questions, which seem to be testing Robert's memory of the story. Why do we do this so often? What do we think we are doing? There are several possibilities:

1 To make sure that the child was paying attention to the story.
2 To test the child's understanding of the story.
3 To finish the story-telling session.
4 To affirm a position of superiority.

One could go on; yet every adult (parent or teacher) asked would, at bottom, be certain that such questions would help a child to understand the story. In this way, adults are often very open about their teaching intentions. And yet it could be argued that in other, more subtle, ways some other more significant teaching and learning is taking place. Let us consider this interaction between Robert and his father more closely and look at what Robert was learning.

First, it can be seen that the father was continually referring Robert to the text (for example in line 9), showing Robert the print he was reading and from which the meaning is gained. Furthermore, he encouraged Robert to join in with the reading. He referred Robert to the pictures (line 20), showing Robert that pictures can be a useful clue in understanding what the text says.

Second, the father made connections between chapter eight, the here and now experience, and other parts of the story which Robert had heard before. Thus Robert was learning that making sense of a text requires drawing on past experiences.

Third, the father made mistakes in his reading; some of them he did not notice but others he did; he was not afraid to admit to them and correct himself. This showed Robert that one does not have to be perfect to be a reader, that it is acceptable to make mistakes and that it is possible to correct oneself without waiting for a better informed other to do so.

Last Robert was offered a model of how to behave as a reader: he was shown which way to turn the pages, where to start and finish, in which direction to read the book, and how to understand the relationship between the printed text and the illustrations.

Robert's father would make no claim at all to know anything about the process of learning to read or how to help young children to become readers. What he was doing was sharing one of his favourite books with his son, a book he loved and wanted his son to love too. Indeed, one might question the suitability of the book for Robert; on the tape there were instances when the subtleties of the text were lost on him (for example 14 and 15). However, the writing of A.A. Milne can be understood at different levels and enjoyed in different ways by different people, surely one of the reasons why it has stood the test of time so well. Robert's bookshelves contain all the classics which were loved by his parents in their childhood. They are teaching him to love books by showing that *they* love books and that loving books is important to them. Robert is lucky, in that his parents have been able to preserve some of their own treasured books. For others, the school and the school library service have important roles to play in opening up access to the wide range of superb literature available to children today. Robert's parents too will have the opportunity to see the almost unimaginable richness of children's literature today, surely one of the most dramatic changes in literacy learning over the last 20 years.

Robert's bedtime experience, as reported here, is just one example of a nightly routine. Nobody would claim that Robert's learning as a reader could be completed in just one session, but the cumulative effect of many story-reading sessions, along with the experience of seeing his parents and others reading for meaning and enjoyment, serve to give Robert a firm basis for his own development as a reader.

Robert was four, nearly of school age, but learning to read does not have to wait so long. The other day I was watching a mother look at a picture book with her young child of about two years old. The mother talked about the pictures before she read the short text which she then elaborated. As she did so she was continually relating what was in the book to the child's own experiences and understanding. In these few short moments that young child, still two years away from any formal instruction or reception class teaching, was having a valuable 'reading lesson'.

I shall now go on to consider how parents' activities as 'reading teachers' continue when children go to school. First, I will take a brief overview of the development of the role of parents in primary education during the last two decades.

Parents in school

In 1982, Margaret Meek described parents as, 'the most natural and most neglected support' of the teacher. It cannot be denied that in primary schools most parents are involved in their child's education to some extent. However, the term 'parental involvement' can mean anything from assistance with fund raising, or help in the classroom, to an active participation in management and decision making.

The days are now long past, let us hope, when a notice on the front door of schools declared, 'Parents not permitted past this point'; the old viewpoint of teachers as enlightened professionals dispensing knowledge to grateful lost ignorant people is at last dying if not completely dead. One might argue that we are in danger of going to the other extreme in these days of parents' rights and the packaging of education as a service provided for the consumers, the parents. The Plowden Report (1967), speaking of the role of parents, said.

> One of the essentials for educational advance is a closer partnership between the two parties to every child's education.

The report went on to argue for schools to increase parental participation as a means of increasing parental interest.

The Bullock Report (1975) put forward the proposition that the working-class child was linguistically under-stimulated at home. Schools were encouraged to involve parents so that the staff would be able to influence working-class parents. Strategies suggested to compensate for this under-stimulation included home visits and courses on language development for secondary children. Parents were to be encouraged to talk and read to their children, but discouraged from any actual teaching. Schools were not encouraged to involve parents in their teaching of reading programmes.

Joan Tough (1977) also advised caution when involving parents. In *Talking and Learning* she said,

...Bringing unpaid, untrained help into schools has its problems and we would not want to give children experiences that were not appropriate and valuable.

This view was often shared by teachers who were keen to protect their professional expertise. The N.U.T. pamphlet 'Parents in Schools' (1979) agreed that parents could be helpful in many ways but doubted the wisdom of involving them in areas which require 'professional skills', particularly with the teaching of reading.

Indeed in April 1985 an article in *The Times Educational Supplement* said, 'The increasingly high profile of parents in more than half the country's primary schools could pose a threat to teachers' status.' The N.A.S./U.W.T. was quoted in the article as saying,

It has always been our view that parents should take a keen interest in their children's education and children progress faster if their parents help to teach them to read. Some parents have always helped to teach their children to read before they start school, but this is far removed from teaching a group of children to read in a classroom situation, which requires the considerable technical expertise of the teacher.

In the light of such discouraging comment it would seem that the idea of involving parents did not have much to commend it to teachers. However, several projects have been undertaken that suggest, very strongly, that parental involvement can be beneficial for all concerned.

Hewison and Tizard (1980), working with seven- and eight-year-old children, investigated whether differences in school achievement within a working-class population could be related to differences in home background. The factor to be most strongly associated with reading success was whether or not the mother regularly heard the child read. It is interesting to note that the vital factor was not whether the mother read to the child but if she heard the child read. The study found that about half the sample of working-class parents spent some time helping their children with the mechanics of reading. Hardly any had discussed this previously with the school and few reported any encouragement from the school.

This study was extended by Tizard, Schofield and Hewison (1982) – the Haringey project – to find if there was a causal relationship between active parental help and reading performance. The sample was divided into three groups; one where children were given no extra help, one where children were regularly heard reading at home and one where the children were given extra help at school from a specially appointed experienced teacher. It was found that those children who read at home showed a significant increase in their reading attainment. The improvements made by those children who received extra professional help at school were not a great as those who read at home. It is worth noting that even when children read to non-English-speaking parents, there was still a significant improvement in reading attainment. The researchers also reported that the parents showed great satisfaction in this form of involvement and the children became more enthusiastic about their reading.

A project which followed on from the Haringey project, described above, was the Belfield Reading Project (Hannon 1981). This began as an attempt to involve parents more systematically and intensively in their children's reading development. The project was intended to build on the work that parents were already doing with their children, and also to enliven and maintain the children's interest in books. Since the latter was the main aim, it was stressed that the parents were not being asked to teach their children to read. However, in reporting the outcomes of their project, the researchers still seem anxious to guard the professional role and traditional sensitivity of the teacher:

> Whilst it would be wrong to conclude that any improvement in the child's attitude or ability in reading was a direct result of this organised parental involvement, there is no doubt that both child and parent gained some benefit... none of the teachers felt that the parents were interfering in any way with the role of the school.

It is almost as if teachers regarded themselves as the professionals who were generous enough to allow the parents a little access into their domain. However, time passes and now it is far more common to hear parents described as 'partners', a label which implies that the roles are different but of equal value. Many parents become uneasy when the teacher assumes an exclusive professional expertise, and only gives them a 'helping' role. It is often feared by teachers that parents will want to push their children on too far and will begin to make unfavourable comparisons between their own and other children. In fact, most work in this area has shown that this is not the case. Parents are normally aware of their own children's capabilities and want the best for them. They are anxious for advice on how best to help their children. Teachers need to remember that parents with their unique relationship with their children have something valuable to contribute to their children's education, as do the teachers, with their professional knowledge. It can only be of benefit if these two influences can work together.

The report carried out for Leeds Education Authority (Alexander 1991) found that home-school links were seen as a low priority at an authority level. However, at school level a number of initiatives were observed, the result of an increased awareness among teachers of the value of parental involvement as well as of recent legislation requiring the greater involvement of parents. Schools have become much more accountable to parents through the requirements of the 1988 Education Reform Act, the spirit of which found expression in the Parents' Charter of 1991. In the 1990s teachers are both motivated and required to make their classroom practice and ideology accessible to parents; so perhaps we can now look forward to a true sharing of information and insights, which can only benefit the child.

There follows a description of a home-school project which took place in one class of a large first school of ten classes, catering for children between the ages of five and nine. The class was a Year 1 class. The school is situated in the centre of a large council estate on the outskirts of a major city. The class teacher, Anne, takes up the description:

The school is a large first school, housed in a modern building. The classrooms are semi-open-plan and classes share art and craft areas. The school is organised on a class basis, divided by age groups. This project was carried out with a class of 33 Year 1 children and their parents.

Previously parental involvement in the school has been very slight. A few of the staff would welcome more but the majority do not feel happy with parents becoming too close. Contact parents have with the school is on a highly organised and infrequent basis. Once a term they are invited to watch their child's class assembly, after which they are invited to stay for a cup of coffee during playtime and talk with the class teacher. One parents' evening is held during the year which is the only formal contact between parents and teachers. Any other contact in encouraged to be made through the headteacher.

The general reading level throughout the school is average to below average. A core reading scheme is used with others slotted in. Children are in the habit of taking their reading books home to practise.

The teaching of reading in my class tends to be much less formal than many others in the school. There is much more talk and reading to the children. The children are encouraged to look for contextual clues and to read with an emphasis on enjoying the story rather than decoding each and every word.

A letter was sent to the parents of all children in my class, inviting them to a special meeting to be held after the class assembly. It was thought that the parents were familiar with coming into school for this and would not be required to make an extra journey. Attendance at the meeting was very good. Two-thirds of the children in the class had at least one parent attend and in several cases both parents were present. This compares with nine parents who attended the last school annual meeting. Most parents said that they thought reading was important and they wanted to know how they could help their children.

The headteacher opened the meeting and explained the project in very general terms. I then described the project in more detail. The main emphasis of the meeting was that the school wanted to work together with the parents. Many of the parents already spent a considerable time helping their children with reading and we felt it would be profitable to link that work with the work we do in school.

The parents were told of my philosophy of reading which in some aspects is somewhat different from that which they had already experienced. I stressed the need for enjoyment of reading and that reading does not necessarily mean progress through a reading scheme. Parents were advised not to put any pressure on their children and to abandon any reading if resistance was shown.

I then explained the practical details of the project. Parents were asked to hear their children read every other day. These would be the days when the child had read to me in school. On the other days the child would not take his reading book home and the parent was asked to read to the child. It was continually emphasised that these reading times should be times for enjoyment, short and relaxed.

Each parent was given a handout which repeated most of what had been said in the meeting. The meeting was then opened for questions and discussion.

The response from parents was favourable and there were no antagonistic reactions. Most parents seemed to feel relieved that their efforts were being endorsed and grateful for the help and support of the school. Questions asked were mainly of a purely practical nature and there was no questioning of the essential basis of the project. Parents were eager to start. The meeting closed with an encouragement to the parents to come into the classroom and discuss their child's reading with me at any time.

Handouts were sent to those parents who had not attended the meeting.

On the whole the reaction to the project was good from all sides. The children were very enthusiastic and were keen to tell their parents what had to be done. They seemed to appreciate having a specific part to read each evening and knowing that what they did at home would be recognised in school the following morning. Previously they had vaguely practised a few pages and some children would read each page several times at home before they had a chance to read it at school.

The majority of parents was involved with the project. Five made no response at all, 18 signed the card but wrote no comment and ten signed the card and made regular comments. In many cases the cards were used as a way of seeking information. Some examples of the comments made are:

She's getting on very well and she really takes an interest in the stories.

I've noticed how well she's doing. She reads all her books with hardly any hesitation.

Matthew gets mixed up on the word 'ate'.

Alan wishes to read more pages to me. So I let him.

He's read to page 17. But he's still not got how to express it.

O.K. Are these books really good for reading?

First, I will examine the response of the parents. It could be claimed that comments were not very forthcoming on the cards and we need to ask why this was so. It could be that some parents were unwillingly to commit themselves to paper. For these parents the written word may not be their most natural form of communication; indeed Anne told me that parents came into the classroom to discuss their child's reading quite frequently. Parents might also have been unsure of what sort of comment to make. They might have felt that what they wanted to say was not a valid point or that they were stating an obvious point. Their natural apprehension at being asked to do something new could have been eased in the initial presentation of the project. The teacher could have been more explicit, giving concrete examples of comments and encouraging parents to write down whatever they felt or noticed, however seemingly trivial. Some parents might be negatively affected by painful memories of their own schooling and feel understandably anxious about writing 'for a teacher' – and about an educational issue, into the bargain.

By far the largest number of comments on the cards were favourable and this could possibly be interpreted as a lack of discrimination by the parents. On the other hand, teachers often emphasise the need for children to be encouraged, to hear feedback on their performance, and to feel a sense of success. Anne herself emphasised 'the need for enjoyment of reading'. Furthermore, parents were beginning to notice differences and improvements in the way their children were reading; for example the comments above show how parents were noticing their children's expression in reading and their enjoyment of the stories.

Anne showed me all the cards and comments which might be described as unfavourable, including those telling the teacher that children were getting muddled up with words, needed more practice etc. It is encouraging that parents were willing to make comments like this to the teacher. On the whole, Anne found that parents did not want to push their child ahead regardless, as she had feared. They did not attempt to cover up for the child and in fact tended to be even stricter than the teacher! Parents were demonstrating that they appreciated that reading is more than a steady plod through a graded reading scheme and that the children must understand what they were doing.

One of the comments which was reported questioned the choice of books, asking 'Are these books really good for reading?' The parent felt that there was too much 'fun' in them, having expected books full of repetition. The teacher invited her to come in for a discussion and showed her how the books could help her son to develop as a reader as well as providing enjoyment and motivation. Without the confidence to take up this opportunity, when it was offered, her questions might have remained unasked. Trust and respect on both sides of the partnership resulted in increased understanding.

In many schools there is already a considerable degree of contact between teachers and parents. However, where there is no such openness, a justifiable reason for contact is appreciated by both parties. Several parents commented favourably on the project and expressed a wish that it would carry on when their children moved into a new class.

This brings me on to a consideration of the impact of such a project on the rest of the school, and the value of an initiative that is not a school-wide project. The other staff of the school showed general interest in the project. However this did not develop into commitment to try it out for themselves. Some of the staff questioned the advisability of involving parents in the teaching of reading. Their anxieties might be met by suggesting that helping parents towards an increased awareness of the reading process and how children can best be helped would make them less confrontational in future contacts with the school. Whole-school developments are unlikely to prosper without whole-staff commitment. But individual teachers, like individual parents and individual children, have the right to a hearing.

The children took a great interest in the project. There was now a link between the reading they did at home and their reading at school. They were able to read more often and to talk with their parents about their reading and the books they had read, certain of shared knowledge and understanding.

If any general conclusion can be drawn from this project, it is that parental involvement in reading can only be beneficial. The benefits of closer co-operation between parents and teachers are mutual and it is vital that the interest both have in the children should be fully exploited. Parents can only go so far in becoming involved in the work of the school; it remains the task of the teacher to create the opportunities for involvement and encourage them. Closer co-operation does not mean diminishing the professional status of the teacher but rather a linking of two different but equally valuable adult roles in the lives of the children.

The next, much briefer, case study looks at a similar way of working with parents in relation to reading, but in a completely different context. This took place in a private pre-preparatory school where the idea of parents as consumers, now beginning to pervade the state education system, is already well established. Parents at this school have no inhibitions at all about expressing their opinions in writing. Here it is practice throughout the school for children to have a reading diary which goes to and from school and home with their reading book. In this teachers, parents and children write about the children's reading progress. I shall look at examples from a brother and sister aged six and three respectively.

Justin

Teacher: 'Captain Bumble' Told me about the story and then read his favourite part. 'Cat on the roof'

Mother: Read all of 'Cat on the roof' – did not seem to have any problems.

Teacher: Told me about the story – seemed to enjoy it – read very well. 'A day in town'

Child: Read all of the book it was very nice and I enjoyed it.

Teacher: I'm very glad you have enjoyed this story Justin. You read very well today. 'The sunflower that went flop'. I think you will enjoy this story – I thought it was quite funny.

Child: I think you were quite right. It *was* funny.

Teacher: Well done, Justin you read very well today. I'm glad you enjoyed the story. 'Singing to the moon' – this has lots of different stories, you will have to let me know which is your favourite.

Mother: Read up to page 15 well, hesitating at the new words but did well in trying to work them out.

Child: In the mouse and the old woman I found two funny words knock and answered which have k and w are silent.

Mother: Read up the end of page 33 – seems to be enjoying the different stories.

Teacher: Well done, Justin – those are quite difficult words aren't they?

Teacher: 'The Wonder Whizz' read to page 6. Some difficult words. Encouraged him to break down words into sound blend 'chunks' to help work them out i.e. th/throt/throttle.

Mother: Finished the story. Managed the 'breakdown' method of putting harder words together very well – got the idea quickly.

Teacher: Read well. Thanks for letting me know about Justin this morning – better to know he is feeling sensitive – normally that sort of comment would not have upset him but spurred him to regain his usual standard! I will be more thoughtful about what I say.

Child: I read the Beautiful pig. I managed breaking up the words too. I liked when they got married.

Mother: Sorry I wasn't able to read the other book with him, unfortunately I'm still bedridden. Justin insisted on making his own comment and with the harder words with the spelling we're breaking them up the same way as we're doing with the reading – he's managing well, is that the right way to do it? Justin's writing seems to have come on very nicely all of sudden?

Teacher: Yes, Justin has progressed a great deal even since Easter!

Don't worry about him reading both books – I hope you are feeling better by now – Justin has been quite concerned about you.

Mother: Read well.

Teacher: Keep 'The Catten' and also 'Lavender the library cat' but don't worry if you don't feel up to both! – he is not going to deteriorate and he reads quite a lot to me in class anyway.

There are several points we can make about these extracts from Justin's reading diary before we go on to look at his sister's. The first thing to note is the confident and fluent tone of all the comments from parent, teacher and child. This parent seems much more confident than the parents described in the previous project, in describing what she does with Justin, although she asks, 'Is this the right way to do it? Yet we must be careful not be deceived by this into thinking that this mother and these parents are necessarily more aware or concerned than the others, simply because they seem to have more confidence in the particular means of expression required by the school.

The enhanced accountability comes across when the teacher apologises to the parent for a remark she had made to the child. I do not know what this was about but it is clear that once the channels of communication are open we must be prepared to accept that they will be used for many purposes. It is interesting to consider who is in control in this journal and who has the greater power in the relationship between home and school. Does this alter the teaching and learning process? Perhaps that is the more negative way of considering the matter. A more positive way would be to say that here is the true partnership of which we have spoken earlier; all three partners have equal and yet different roles and all are working together to help Justin to develop as a reader.

The phrase 'read well' is used frequently in the diary by both teacher and parent and yet no form of definition or explanation is given. Does it mean that all the words were correctly decoded, or that the story was read fluently with expression and understanding? We do not know. What is perhaps more crucial is that we do not know whether all those using the phrase meant the same thing by it. It important to clarify terms and criteria when entering into a partnership so that participants can share their common understandings.

Note that once the idea of 'breaking down' words is introduced by the teacher, it is constantly referred to by both parent and child. We need to beware of this and ensure that we continually emphasise the need for flexibility and adaptability in the use of strategies for making sense of a text. There will be occasions when the 'breaking down' strategy does not work, and may even make decoding more difficult. The teacher's desire to offer the mother 'helpful' strategies may have unforeseen effects.

Finally a great sense of urgency comes through when the mother reports that she is unable to read two books with the child each night. The teacher attempts to reassure her, but her use of words such as 'deteriorate' and the emphasis that Justin reads a lot at school, may serve to increase mother's feeling of pressure. The teacher seems to be reinforcing the need for continuous progress which, it is implied, can only come through regular monitored reading. If the mother falls down on her part of the bargain, the teacher seems to suggest, the school will have to compensate.

We can see if similar points emerge from the reading diary of Justin's three year old sister, Danielle. This contains comments by the teacher, the nursery nurse and the parent.

Danielle

Teacher: 'How do I put it on?' In school Danielle was paying very close attention to the print and was 'reading' along with me. We looked particularly at 'c' at the start of cap.

Mother: Danielle also recognises 'D' at the start of Do as the same as the start of her own name.

Teacher: Nov 21. Danielle says that Justin has read this to her. She read the whole book to me straightaway with a high level of accuracy. I was really pleased with this. Point to the words as she reads so that she focusses on the details of the print.

Mother: I asked Justin about reading this to Danielle and apparently he has – some time ago in 'after-care' – she too has surprised me with her level of accuracy, she has enjoyed it very much and so have I, to hear her reading it so well – a good memory maybe?

Teacher: That's great – a good memory is the start of good reading! In the middle of the puddle. A more complex text but with lots of repetition. See how Danielle gets on reading it with you.

Mother: Danielle seemed to struggle with this book, we've read to page 20 and she got tired with it, looking at the pictures and repeating after me but not actually looking at the words that I pointed to.

Teacher: 'The grand old Duke of York'. Danielle and I sang this together! Because she knows the rhyme well she is able to 'read' with a high degree of accuracy. Encouraging her to point will help her make the connection between the print and the words.

Mother: Went through the book with her, pointing at the words as we went along. On the last page she knew the words 'down' and 'up' when I pointed to them but when I asked her to find them for me, she couldn't.

Teacher: 'The Park, the park'. In school today Danielle was joining in with me and at times she was able to take over. See how she gets on at home.

Mother: Dannie seemed to struggle with this book. On several pages she seemed to read the whole sentence completely right – then with the same words on the next page she didn't know them!

Teacher: Don't worry too much about that. At this stage children tend to use the pictures and the sense of the story as cues for what the print says rather than the actual words themselves. What is more important is that they are following the continuity of the story. In time Danielle will gradually come to pay more attention to the details of the words e.g. initial letters. What Danielle was doing probably indicated that on some pages of the book the text related well to the picture and on other pages there is little connection!

The first thing to note in discussion of Danielle's reading diary is that there are far fewer parental contributions. It can be seen that the comments which are made by the mother are more concerned with Danielle 'reading' by herself rather than her reading along with an adult. Here is an indication of a common view that only when a child reads fluently and independently is it a 'real' reading. This can often be the cause of confusion and misunderstanding when parents and teachers talk together about children's reading. Their use of the basic term 'reading' needs to be clarified at the outset of any partnership in this area of a child's learning.

Note too the way in which the parental comments focus on the subordinate skills of reading. Danielle's mother notices her letter and sound matching and her recognition of individual words. It is as if these identifiable skills are something concrete for parents to refer to, by which progress can be measured; they may seem more precise, more accurate or more informative than the rather nebulous concept of 'apprenticeship reading'.

Finally there is a confusion between memory and reading. A remark which is frequently heard by teachers is, 'She's not really reading it, she's just remembering it.' The process of reading is an extremely complex one and particularly at the very early stages it is difficult to specify exactly what is going on. Teachers who embark on partnership and strive for shared understanding, can show parents the importance of remembering words in context first, before recognising them out of context. They can demonstrate the move from the specific recall to the more general. They can reassure parents that it really is reading, not cheating, as they might have been taught themselves at the ages of five and six.

Literacy and culture

So far in our discussion of 'literacy beyond teachers' we have looked at children whose first language is the language of the school and whose prior experience at home has to a greater or lesser extent overlapped with some of the literacy experiences and expectations of the school. I now, although briefly, consider the literacy learning of those children whose first language is not English, and whose literacy experiences are different in some respects from those they find in school.

Hilary Minns (1990) tells the story of Gurdeep's introduction to school and how he made sense of his literacy experiences at home and those he encountered in the classroom. As Minns says,

> Gurdeep has been surrounded by several quite different literacy practices in his home ever since he was a baby. These practices are embedded in the set of institutions and relations that form his culture: the religious life of his family and community and the domestic life, work and leisure occupations of those around him. (p.7)

To Gurdeep literacy was an important part of his Sikh culture and the sacred text had power and influence over his family and friends. For them this text, and the telling of folk tales with a strong moral, were ways of maintaining contact with their religious and cultural traditions.

Sumant is a secondary mathematics teacher who was born in a small village in rural India where he lived before moving to England at the age of four. I talked to him about his early memories of spoken language, reading and writing and the part that literacy played in his upbringing. Sumant speaks:

I didn't go to school in India but I remember that in the village there was a building with two rooms. That was the school. The younger children went to one room and the older ones up to about 13 went to the other. When they got to 13 that was it, the end of their education.

There was nothing in English in our home; the only print in the house was in Hindi. There were no magazines or newspapers but just religious books containing tales and folk lore. They were for the older generation, I don't remember anything for the children. My uncle was the teacher in the school but he didn't have any books for children. He used a blackboard but mainly I think it was just from memory.

My grandfather used to tell us lots of stories about his own past and often he would sing folk tales to us. When it was hot we would sleep outside and I can remember lying in the heat, falling asleep and listening to my grandfather singing. We spoke Gujerati at home; nobody spoke any English.

When I was four we came to Preston in England. My father had come earlier and my mother and I followed on later. I think the first English I ever heard spoken was on the plane. We went to live at my great-uncle's house; he had two younger children and two older children already there.

We arrived at a weekend and by the end of the next week I was in school I can remember my father taking me on the first day. It was a nursery class which was part of an infant school. There weren't a lot of other Indians in the school – about 30% I should think. I didn't recognise anything that happened in school – it was all different and strange.

I spoke Gujerati with my parents and older relations but all the children in the family spoke in English. I used my intuition to work out what they were saying, by the way they spoke and the way they moved their hands.

I remember the comics when I first came to England – Dandy and Beano. I loved those and I could understand them because the pictures told the story.

In school I was really in the same position as all the other kids; they didn't know anything either – only I couldn't speak the language. I learned the alphabet and my cousins helped me to spell my name. At home we had a newspaper in Gujerati and also the religious books in Hindi.

On Saturday mornings I went to school to learn to read and write in Gujerati. I went for about a month but it was impossible. There were about 100 kids in one room all sitting at desks and one teacher. Later the teacher from that school came as a lodger in our house and he taught me the

Gujerati alphabet by rote. I can't read in Gujerati now. I didn't try to read the books at home because they were just full of words with no pictures to help.

After Year 1 in school I wasn't put into Year 2 but I went into another class for those who were having problems with the language. They were mostly Indian children and some English children who were slow. I hated that and it really put me out. I'm sure that it put me back in my schooling rather than helped. The teachers didn't realise that a lot of Indian children learn by their wits and they were taking them away from all the English speaking other children so made it more difficult for them to learn.

My parents didn't help me with my learning at home because they believed it was the school's job. I think a lot of Indians believe that the ability to learn is inherent – that it will just happen and you can't do anything to help it. I'll certainly help and encourage my child to learn though and I've noticed that the parents who were born in this country, or who have been here a long time like me are the ones who come to parents' evening; the older ones don't see the need.

As time passed I spoke more and more English. The older relatives insisted that we speak in Gujerati, I think they felt it was a way of maintaining a link with India. All the younger generation spoke English though. I speak to my parents in Gujerati now. They can understand English very well now and speak it quite well too. If there is a complicated idea or concept they don't have the English to grasp it though.

I think the language is an important part of the cultural heritage and I want my child to grow up being able to speak Gujerati.

Any discussion of Sumant's account of his childhood experiences must, of course, take into account the fact that he is describing events that took place 25 years ago; memories can, of course, be affected by time. However, there are some important points which can confidently be made in the light of the relationship between culture and literacy learning.

First the importance of story comes across very strongly. Storytelling played a central role in Sumant's childhood and was a means of passing on both family history and cultural and religious understandings. When Sumant arrived in school here there was nothing familiar to him, certainly no familiar stories. These days teachers have much more access to stories from other cultures, to dual language texts and to audio tapes of stories read in other languages. It would help the transition so much for a young child to hear something familiar. Storytelling can also be used as a bridge into the culture of the classroom and the importance of story in the literacy learning process has been well established.

The importance of the social context of the classroom as a vehicle for literacy learning has also been stressed; Sumant too perceives this as being important, and felt it wrong that he was deprived of this in order to receive extra help in English. It is often the case that when children are having difficulties, or are inexperienced in a particular area, we remove them from a context where they will be among competent literacy users and teach them alone. The strength of peer support and the literacy of the daily classroom routine and environment must not be underestimated.

Sumant loved looking at comics and found them helpful in learning English. We must be as flexible and varied as we can in the materials we use. So often material which is at a suitable reading level is of an insultingly inappropriate interest level.

Finally we need to be aware of the esteem in which the printed word is held in many cultures. Often it is closely bound up with religious practices and the 'sacred word' is treated with reverence. In Sumant's home the only books were those containing religious stories. Books were for adults, not for children and were certainly not seen as 'fun'. This is all very different from the ways in which printed books are used in schools, and from the irreverent use of language found in many children's books.

Conclusion

In this chapter I have explored some aspects of the wider context of literacy learning, and the relationship between the classroom and the community. It has been recognised that literacy learning takes place in many ways outside school and I have considered how this learning is accommodated into the school context. I have argued that the culture of the classroom, within which a particular classroom literacy is created, comes through the interaction of a variety of different perspectives on both literacy and learning. The hierarchical power relationships of the classroom will, if not carefully monitored, inequitably determine what is valued and accepted and what is rejected; it is the responsibility of the teacher to ensure that the understandings and competencies of all members of the community have a part in a common classroom literacy.

CHAPTER EIGHT

Conclusion

The Introduction to this book began by raising two questions – What is literacy? and How is literacy best developed? These questions are returned to as the focus of this concluding chapter. In the course of the book we have explored literacy behaviours of many different types. Some are more commendable than others and provide evidence of teachers who are empowering children by giving them strategies for using print. In all the examples, however, it must be said, teachers were doing their very best for the children in their care, by adopting those approaches which to them seemed most suitable. Has a definition of literacy been reached and have the best ways of developing literacy been identified?

Bruner, (1986) describes children as creators of 'possible worlds' and so Dyson (1987) argues the need for allowing children 'building space'. In order for effective learning to take place, children need opportunities for those social interactions which, in Vygotsky's terms (1978) develop into 'individual reflection'. Any exploration of literacy in classrooms needs to take into account the culture of the classroom, for the influence of that culture on how literacy will be learned will be strong. Cook-Gumperz (1986) says,

> Literacy has become redefined within the context of schooling and has turned into what we now refer to as schooled literacy, that is, a system of decontextualised knowledge validated through test performances.' (p.41)

Official definitions of literacy are inextricably linked with schooling. Despite the work of Scribner and Cole (1981), where they found that, among the Vai people in Liberia, literacy and schooling developed as two separate activities, in the cultural context of a late twentieth century British primary school the two are rarely, if ever, differentiated. Schooling is seen by some as the transmission of knowledge and the relationship between teaching and learning is a close one – children learn what they are taught. Schools are thought to own literacy and this view of children as passive learners gives expectations of what happens in classrooms.

At the time of writing the English National Curriculum orders are to be re-written and, if reports are to be believed, it is to become more prescriptive and firmer in its definition of what is 'correct'. It would seem that 'correctness' is a notion to be applied in all contexts, so that standard English is to become the language of the playground. *The Case for Revising the Order* (NCC 1992) says,

> The current order does not, however, place sufficient emphasis on the requirement that all pupils (irrespective of the level towards which they are working) should become confident users of standard English. (para.34)

Here surely is an example of the idea that what is taught in school is what is learned and that literacy and schooling are inextricably linked.

As we have seen elsewhere, success in schooling means not only knowing how to do things, but demonstrating this knowledge in the correct contexts. Learning, however, while maybe including that aspect, is something different. Vygotsky's (1978) concept of 'interiorization' in which 'every function in the child's cultural development appears twice, first on the social level, and later, on the individual level' (p.57) is relevant here. In relation to a definition of classroom literacy and the question of what counts as valid literacy learning within a classroom, I have argued throughout this book that children's learning takes place as they appropriate for themselves those aspects of literate behaviours that are learned socially. However, in that process of appropriation, other influences, experiences and understandings come to modify the 'official' definition of literacy.

Negotiation of literacy

In the first chapter a reception teacher, called Sue, described the changes in her thinking which led her to give greater freedom and responsibility to the children, particularly in their writing. An observation during the early period of the change in Sue's class illustrates how classrooms are places where a continual process of negotiation takes place. McDermott (1977) argues that relations between teachers and children may help or hinder learning and that a system of trusting relationships is used by both to make sense of each other. This is done through a process of mutual negotiation, part of which will be, of necessity, some form of modification of the 'official' definition of literacy.

Faye

It was Faye's first day in the reception class, along with seven other children. Faye was just five and had spent two terms in a nursery class. Sue had set out a variety of tabletop activities, selected for their immediate appeal to the children. As Sue said, 'I'm very concerned that they should all have a lovely first day.' The activities included bright green dough, sand, large and small bricks, peg boards, writing and drawing materials, stickle bricks, bead threading and a listening centre on which was a story tape. All the new children, except for one, went straight to the table where the teacher was sitting ready to write for the children to copy. Sue's interpretation of this was that the children often expected to get down to 'serious work' in the infants and felt that writing fulfilled their expectations. The children were told to draw a picture of something they had received as a Christmas present. Faye was very tentative in her drawing. She picked up a crayon, apparently at random, and made light very spidery marks on the paper. She continually watched the other children and looked around the room, keeping a check on the whereabouts of the teacher. Gradually she became more confident and her drawing became stronger. Sue came to talk to Faye about her drawing and after a short discussion she wrote a sentence underneath the picture in yellow felt pen; this was not dictated by Faye but was a paraphrase of what had been said in the discussion. Sue then asked Faye, 'Would you like to trace over my writing or go underneath it – you can choose?' Faye chose to trace; the teacher held her hand as she traced the first few letters with a pencil and then said, 'Go on, you carry on now, that's ever so good, you're starting all the letters in the right place.'

The children had been given the opportunity for choice. They chose to go to the writing table and take part in the activity specified there and Faye was given the choice of how to copy the teacher's writing. However, all these choices were set out by the teacher and took place within clear constraints imposed by the teacher. The children had choice of all the activities in the classroom but once they had made the choice of writing, the element of choice decreased dramatically. The teacher had retained ownership of this typical school-centred literacy act. The importance placed on the literacy activity, as defined and presented by the teacher, indicated the value which it is given in this classroom culture.

This incident took place at the very start of Faye's career in the reception class; from it she began to learn what it meant to be a pupil in that class. Her initial hesitancy could well be interpreted as a search for appropriate behaviour. It would seem that within this event both Faye and Sue were establishing their roles as teacher and pupil and defining what is appropriate behaviour for each within these roles. There would seem to be an element of negotiation taking place as identities were clarified.

In this incident the negotiation was initiated by the teacher as she offered a choice to Faye. However, the choice was extremely narrow; Faye was presented with two options for performing a tightly-defined task. The teacher had initiated and controlled the activity throughout, even to the extent of determining the degree of negotiation. This activity remained firmly in the ownership and control of the teacher, even when Faye had chosen her method for copying the teacher's writing. It would seem, however, that the children were aware of this control over their learning and in a way accepted it; they also had firm expectations of the roles of teacher and pupil. Faye seemed unsure how to respond when given the relatively open task of drawing a picture of a Christmas present; her tentativeness and her seeking for reassurance of the teacher's presence would seem to support this interpretation. The extent of negotiation was so limited that one wonders what would have happened if the child had made a response which the teacher had deemed to be inappropriate. Having made her choice of tracing, Faye was not left to execute it for herself but Sue maintained her ownership in a very visible and physical way by actually holding Faye's pencil with her as she traced. In this way it was made very clear that there was only one correct way of doing it and Faye was left in no doubt that she could be either right or wrong. The teacher's verbal feedback also was about 'doing it right', serving powerfully to underline the message Faye was receiving. The fact that she continued to respond in what was deemed a 'correct' way does not lessen the degree of strictness of the criteria being applied. The teacher was assessing the response according to clear specifications of what was required for the 'official' literacy of the classroom.

As she began to view the children's literacy understandings and behaviours more positively, Sue began to recognise the extent of the control she exercised over their learning. On one occasion the children had all started making books for themselves by folding over sheets of scrap paper, stapling them in the middle and then drawing and writing in them. Sue reported this to me when I was visiting the school one day, with the comment, 'It's interesting how the pictures are on one side and the writing on the other, isn't it. I wonder if it's indoctrination!' She was referring to the fact that she had always given children pieces of paper which had been folded in half and asked them to draw first on the left hand side and then write on the right. In recognising this pattern, Sue was beginning to understand that there could be other valid responses and she stopped insisting on this routine, allowing the children to choose which they did first and to decide for themselves how they arranged the work on the page. It was in this acknowledgement of the children's competencies and a letting-go of her control that more genuine negotiations began to take place.

Ownership of literacy

The next observation was also recorded in Sue's classroom, five months after the incident with Faye; several changes had taken place within the classroom resulting from Sue's developing perceptions of literacy. The children's own mark-making was now recognised as writing and no longer did the children go through the stages of tracing, undercopying and copying. They 'wrote' their stories, and then read them to Sue, who discussed them with the children. A 'writing table' was now a permanent feature of the classroom and available to the children at all times; it held different sorts of paper, pencils, pens, etc. The ethos of the classroom was now one of acceptance of the children's own work, where risk taking was encouraged and 'mistakes' viewed as positive indications of growing understanding and a search for meaning.

Grant had been painting a picture and wanted to put his name on it and stick it up on the wall. He approached the teacher with a pencil and asked her to write his name for him. She replied that he could write it himself. Grant wrote a backwards 'G' 'Ꮆ' and then said that he did not know what came next. The teacher wrote an 'r' and then handed the pencil back to him. Grant then wrote a 't' and went away, well satisfied, to put his picture on the wall.

The function of this activity was the labelling of the painting and both Sue and Grant understood this. The literacy learning which took place was embedded within this genuine purpose. The final result, although not conventionally 'correct', was appropriate for the purpose and this was recognised by teacher and pupil. The process of negotiation which took place during this event reveals the collaboration between teacher and pupil. Grant initiated the process; he had a specific purpose in mind. It would seem that his initial intention in asking Sue to write his name for him was to get it done as quickly as possible but Sue's response passed the responsibility back to him. She recognised Grant as the owner of this piece of literacy and in leaving the writing to him, showed that she viewed his literacy behaviours as valid. Her subsequent actions provided the necessary support and encouragement, though without taking control. It was Grant who decided that the final product was satisfactory and served the intended purpose. Throughout the incident, the teacher was allowing Grant to take the lead, but providing input when necessary.

A view of literacy as a specified body of knowledge with a linear and hierarchical development of understandings and skills, suggests that all literacy learning is measurable and identifiable. However, as has been seen from the case studies in this chapter and elsewhere, this view does not necessarily account for all the literacy learning that takes place. A view of literacy learning as a cyclical process that takes the child's understandings as the starting point for development, requires the teacher to work within a mutually accepted purpose for the activity.

This latter approach to literacy learning places many more demands on the teacher for it requires a recognition of all the literacy learning which takes place both within and outside the classroom. This cannot be an easy task for a busy teacher. It has become clear that understanding the nature of classroom literacy is not a straightforward process. It must involve exploration of the relationships, interactions and strategies adopted by the pupils and teachers. Taylor (1983) says, when discussing how best to facilitate literacy learning in school,

> Only when children have had the opportunity to inventively construct literate language uses which make sense to them will they be able to participate fully in literate society. (p.93)

To describe literacy learning as a reactive process implies that negotiation takes place and that teacher and pupils are developing and learning together in a state of mutual dependence. The children will take from the teacher's knowledge and resources and the teacher will take from the children's experiences and understandings. In order to 'let the child lead' (Clay 1988), however, a teacher needs insights into what is actually happening in terms of literacy learning during classroom activity.

Re-creation of literacy

The final example from Sue's classroom shows how a teacher's understanding of literacy will strongly influence the children's literate behaviours within the classroom. In this classroom children were allowed freedom to own their own literacy experiences and thus to respond to experience, to choose their mode of response and to manipulate conventions for their own purposes.

In the classroom was a music table on which were a variety of tuned and untuned instruments and a selection of song books. The teacher had written on large cards several of the class's favourite songs, including simple musical notation. The class had been introduced to this notation as a way of remembering and writing down tunes and the children frequently went and experimented at this table. Andy had been working at the writing table and had drawn a rainbow. He showed this to the teacher and after a short conversation she suggested that he might like to write a story about it. After a while Andy returned with the text shown in figure 8.1.

Figure 8.1

Andy told the teacher that he had written the 'rainbow song'. He had chosen the subject of his story, he had chosen the mode in which he would respond (rejecting the teacher's suggestion of writing a story) and he had chosen the literacy convention which he deemed to be most appropriate for his purposes. Andy truly owned that piece of work. The organisation of the classroom, the resources available, and the relationship between teacher and pupils meant that Andy was able to work in this way. The teacher's positive view of children as literacy learners allowed Andy to make that work his very own and to view it as a valuable piece of literacy behaviour and learning.

Throughout this book the social nature of classroom literacy has been emphasised. It has become clear that literacy cannot be defined as a clearly recognisable body of knowledge with identifiable levels of attainment and expected behaviours. It has also been found that the term 'literacy event' is not adequate to describe all the literacy learning which takes place within a classroom. To consider this learning only in terms of specific 'literacy events' is to miss much that is valuable. It would seem therefore that classroom literacy cannot be considered in terms of products; it is more appropriate to think of it in terms of a process. This process is a social one, in that the interaction between the participants influences what counts as valid literacy learning within the classroom and plays a large part in its creation.

In the discussion of this social process of literacy learning, the themes of ownership, negotiation and re-creation have often been used. These themes can be related to Rowland's view of the nature of teaching (1987) which is based on an epistemological understanding. Thus the nature of ownership of literacy learning refers not so much to control of the learners but rather to control of the learning. To own a learning experience means that the language used, the concepts explored and the problem-solving strategies adopted are decided by the owner and thus based on the owner's perception of the experience and the appropriateness of the experience to existing understandings. Thus, as Rowland states, the nature of teaching is changed and the element of negotiation becomes an essential part, for there is,

> ... the assumption that learning is a process of construction or re-construction by the learner and that therefore teaching, which is a deliberate intervening in the learning

> process, must be founded upon an attempt to understand
> the learner's present state of knowledge. (p.122)

Therefore negotiation is not a strategy for gaining control but for understanding the perceptions held by the participants of the nature of literacy learning which is valid within a classroom. Much of that literacy learning will come about as the learners re-create for themselves a literacy which is relevant and purposeful for them within their particular social situation.

Perspectives on literacy

Throughout the analysis and discussion in this book the influence of the teacher's theoretical perspective on literacy has been analysed. A skills-based model of literacy gives responsibility for the teaching to the teacher; s/he teaches the children the skills necessary to break into the body of knowledge known as literacy; terms such as 'word attack skills' underline this view. A view of literacy as part of the continuum of language learning means that children's attempts at making sense of print are viewed positively and encouraged.

The theoretical perspective on literacy held by a teacher also has implications for the provision of resources. A hierarchical linear developmental view of progression in reading, for example, means moving from 'simpler' to a 'harder' book with a larger amount of smaller print, more complex language structures and fewer pictures. Progression is from the simple to the complex; it is the task of the teacher to match the resources to the perceived abilities of the child. In contrast, a 'whole language' approach to literacy learning (Goodman 1979) places the text in a central position. A text is selected on the basis of how far it allows a child to behave as a reader by enabling him/her to make full use of existing language knowledge to gain meaning, and by giving enjoyment through the story (Meek 1988). The classroom also becomes a resource for literacy learning; opportunities and materials are provided. Literacy becomes an integral part of classroom activity with all the participants engaged in relevant literacy activities.

Closely linked to this theoretical perspective on literacy, is a view of children as active and social learners. A teacher who acknowledges the social nature of learning will foster collaboration in the classroom. Reading and writing will become shared activities with meaning and purpose the motivating forces.

There is a dilemma for teachers when their theoretical perspective on literacy learning is not compatible with the view of learning imposed on them from external bodies. This is the dilemma with which many teachers are attempting to come to terms during the present time of debate. However, a view of children as active learners can impose on methodology and resources which come from a different perspective. The relationship which is established between teacher and pupil can be a positive encouraging one and give access to the riches of literacy.

Literacy which children already know

Children enter school as very competent language users and with wide and varied experiences of how print works. For some children this existing knowledge is not recognised and their experience sometimes seems in conflict with the expectations of the classroom. For others their understanding is used and extended within the classroom; they are given confidence in themselves as literacy users. Tizard and Hughes (1984) identified this dichotomy between understandings, 'School learning may become increasingly separated from any learning which takes place outside the classroom.' (p.136) Heath (1983) also describes how the children of Trackton found that their literacy within the community was not valued in the school.

The implication of this lies in the teacher recognising and valuing the learning which takes place outside the classroom and attempting to re-create it within the classroom and also encouraging parents and members of the community to become involved in school life. The benefits of these approaches in terms of literacy learning are well documented (e.g. Jackson and Hannon 1981, Tizard et al 1982).

A child-centred philosophy can result in the 'normalisation' of children and of the learning process. The curriculum is planned with the idea of a 'norm' or a 'normal child' in mind. The teacher is thought of as the provider of a stimulating environment and activities; individual children respond to this in their own way and the teacher steps in at the end to evaluate the learning. Rowland (1987) criticises this 'exploratory model' for failing to recognise the social nature of learning and also for failing to provide children with new ways of thinking which might help them in their learning. If children are to own the curriculum fully, the teacher has to become a learner alongside them. The children control the language and concepts used and the teacher presents the challenges and creates the need.

And so it is that literacy learning is developed in a way which gives children the power and control over their own responses and allows them to create meanings from what they see and hear. It seems to me that meaning is the essence of what we are saying when we talk about literacy. Meaning is at the centre of all: the process of literacy teaching is one of enabling children to continue to behave as 'meaning makers'.

Bibliography

Alexander, R. (1991) *Primary Education in Leeds: Twelfth and final report from the primary needs independent evaluation project* (Leeds: University of Leeds).

Alexander, R., Rose, J. and Woodhead, C. (1992) *Curriculum organisation and classroom practice in primary schools* (London: HMSO).

Anderson, Alonso and Stokes (1984) 'Social and institutional influences on the development and practice of literacy' in Goelman, Oberg and Smith (ed.) *Awakening to Literacy* (London: Heinemann Educational Books).

Bennett, J. (1982) *Learning to Read with Picture Books* (Stroud: Thimble Press).

Berger, P. and Luckman, T. (1966) *The Social Construction of Reality: a treatise in the sociology of knowledge* (Harmondsworth: Penguin).

Bettelheim, B. and Zelan, K. (1981) *On Learning to Read: The Child's Fascination with Meaning* (London: Thames and Hudson).

Bloome, D. (1986) *Beyond Access: an ethnographic study of reading in a culturally diverse inner city school* Paper presented at World Congress of Reading, London.

Board of Education (1931) *Primary Education* (London: HMSO).

Brice Heath, S. (1983) *Ways with Words* (Cambridge: Cambridge University Press).

Bruner, J. (1968) *Towards a Theory of Instruction* (New York: Norton)

Bruner, J. (1986) *Actual Minds, Possible Words* (Harvard: Harvard University Press).

Bruner, J. and Haste, H. (1987) *Making Sense: the child's construction of the world* (London: Methuen).

Butler, A. and Turbill, J. (1984) *Towards a Reading-Writing Classroom* (Rozelle, NSW: Primary English Teaching Association).

Central Advisory Council for Education (1967) *Children and their Primary Schools* (London: HMSO).

Clark, M. (1976) *Young Fluent Readers* (London: Heinemann).

Clark, M. (1988) *New Directions in the Study of Reading* (Basingstoke: Falmer Press).

Clay, M.M. (1979) *Reading: the patterning of complex behaviour* (London: Heinemann).

Clay, M.M. (1982) *Observing Young Readers* (London: Heinemann).

Clay, M.M. (1988) 'Let the children lead' Paper presented at Manchester Literacy Conference.

Cook-Gumperz, J. (ed.) (1986) *The Social Construction of Literacy* (Cambridge: Cambridge University Press).

166

Department of Education and Science (1975) *A language for Life* (London: HMSO).

Department of Education and Science (1982) *Education 5 to 9: an illustrative account of 80 first schools in England* (London: HMSO).

Department of Education and Science (1988) *Report of the Committee of Inquiry into the teaching of English language* (London: HMSO).

Department of Education and Science (1988) *English for Ages 5 to 11* (London: HMSO).

Dombey, H. (1991) 'The sattable and the unsattable: giving our children the assessment in literacy that they deserve.' in Harrison, C. and Ashworth, E. (eds) *Celebrating Literacy, Defending Literacy* (Oxford: Basil Blackwell).

Donaldson, M. (1978) *Children's Minds* (London: Fontana).

Dyson, A.H. (1987) 'The value of time-off tasks: young children's spontaneous talk and deliberate text' *Harvard Educational Review* **57** (4).

Eisner, E. (1982) *Cognition and Curriculum: a basis for deciding what to teach* (London: Longman).

Ferreiro, E. and Teberosky, A. (1983) *Literacy Before Schooling* (London: Heinemann Educational Books).

Freire, P. (1970) *Pedagogy of the Oppressed* (New York: Seabury Press).

Galton, M. and Simon, B. (1980) *Progress and Performance in the Primary School* (London: Routledge and Kegan Paul).

Gee, J. (1990) *Social Linguistics and Literacies* (Basingstoke: Falmer Press).

Gentry, J.R. (1987) *Spel...is a four letter word* (Leamington Spa: Scholastic).

Goelman, H., Oberg, A., and Smith, F. (eds) 1984 *Awakening to Literacy* (London: Heinemann Educational Books).

Goodman, K., Goodman, Y. and Burke, C. (1978) 'Reading for Life: the psycholinguistic basis' in Hunter-Grundin, E. and Grundin, H. (eds) *Reading: Implementing the Bullock Report* (London: Ward Lock Educational).

Goodman, K. and Goodman, Y.(1979) 'Learning to read is natural' in Resnick, L. and Weaver, P. (eds) *Theory and Practice of Early Reading* (Hillsdale, N.J.: Lawrence Erlbaum).

Gorman, T., and Fernandes, C. 1992 *Reading in Recession* (Windsor: NFER).

Graff, H. (1987) *The Labyrinths of Literacy: Reflections on Literacy Past and Present* (New York: Falmer).

Gray, W.S. (1956) *The Teaching of Reading and Writing* (Paris: U.N.E.S.C.O.).

Hall, N. (1987) *The Emergence of Literacy* (Sevenoaks: Hodder and Stoughton).

Hall, N. (1989) *Writing with Reason* (Sevenoaks: Hodder and Stoughton).

Halliday, M. (1978) *Language as a social semiotic* (London: Edward Arnold).

Hargreaves, D. (1972) *Interpersonal relations and education* (London: Routledge and Kegan Paul).

Harste, J., Woodward, V. and Burke, C. (1984) *Language Stories and Literacy Lessons* (Portsmouth, New Hampshire: Heinemann Educational Books).

Hewison, J. and Tizard, S. (1980) 'Parental involvement and reading attainment' *British Journal of Educational Psychology* **50** 209-15.

HMI (1990) *The Teaching and Learning of Reading in Primary Schools* (London: HMSO).

Holdaway, D. (1979) *The Foundation of Literacy* (Sydney: Ashton Scholastic).

Holdaway, D. (1980) *Independence in reading* (Sydney: Ashton Scholastic).

Hymes, D. (1972) 'Models of the interactions of language and social life' in Gumperz, J. and Hymes, D. (eds) *Directions in Sociolinguistics: the ethnography of communication* (New York: Holt Rinehart).

ILEA (1989) *The Primary Language Record* (London: Centre for Language in Primary Education).

Ingham, J. (1981) *Books and reading development* (London: Heinemann Educational Books).

Jackson, A. and Hannon, P. (1981) *The Belfield Reading Project* (Rochdale: Belfield Community Council).

Jackson, M. (1987) 'Making sense of school' in Pollard, A. (ed) *Children and their primary schools* (Lewes: Falmer Press).

Johnson, L. and O'Neill, C. (1985) *Dorothy Heathcote's collected writings on education and drama* Hutchinson.

Katz, L. (1987) 'What should young children be doing? *The Wingspread Journal* **9** (2).

Lake, M. (1991) 'Surveying all the factors: Reading Research.' in *Language and Learning* 6 8-13.

Langer, J. (1986) *Language, Literacy and Culture: issues of society and schooling* (Norwood: Ablex).

Martin, T. (1989) *The Strugglers* (Milton Keynes: Open University Press).

McKenzie, M. (1986) *Journeys into Literacy* (Schofield and Sims).

McDermott, R.P. (1977) 'Social relations as contexts for learning in school' *Harvard Educational Review* Vol 47 No 2.

Meek, M. (1982) *Learning to Read* (London: The Bodley Head).

Meek, M. (1983) *Achieving Literacy* (London: Routledge and Kegan Paul).

Meek, M. (1988) *How Texts Teach What Readers Learn* (Lewes: Falmer).

Meek, M. (1991) *On Being Literate* (London: The Bodley Head).

Minns, H. (1990) *Read it to me now!* (London: Virago).

National Curriculum Council (1992) *National Curriculum English: The case for Revising the Order*.

Oxenham, J. (1980) *Literacy: Writing, Reading and Social Organisation* (London: Routledge and Kegan Paul).

Paley, V.G. (1981) *Wally's Stories* (Cambridge: Mass.: Harvard University Press).

Paley, V.G. (1986) 'On listening to what the children say' *Harvard Educational Review* **56** (2).

Pearson, H. (1987) *Children becoming Readers* (Basingstoke: Macmillan Education).

Pollard, A. (1985) *The Social World of the Primary School* (Eastbourne: Holt, Rinehart and Winston).

Pollard, A. and Tann, S. (9187) *Reflective Teaching in the Primary School* (London: Cassell).

Rogers, C. (1969) *Freedom to Learn* (Oxford: Merrill).

Rowland, S. (1987) 'Child in control: towards an interpretive model of teaching and learning' in Pollard, A. *Children and their Primary Schools* (Lewes: Falmer Press).

Schiefflin and Cochran-Smith (1984) 'Learning to read culturally: literacy before schooling' in Goelman et al op cit.

Schofield, W. (1979) *Haringey Reading Project* Final Report to DES.

Scollon and Scollon (1979) *Linguistic Convergence: an ethnography of speaking at Fort Chipewyan Alberta* (New York: Academic Press).

168

Scribner, S. and Cole, M. (1981) *The Psychology of Literacy* (Cambridge: Mass.: Harvard University Press).

Smith, D. (1983) 'Reading and writing in the real world: explorations into the culture of literacy' in Parker, R. and Davis, F.(ed) *Developing literacy: young children's use of language* (International Reading Association).

Smith, F. (1978) *Reading* (Cambridge: Cambridge University Press).

Smith, F. (1983) *Essays into Literacy* (London: Heinemann).

Southgate-Booth, V., Arnold, H. and Johnson, H. (1981) *Extending Beginning Reading* (London: Heinemann).

Tamburrini, J. (1986) 'Trends in developmental research and their implications for infant school education: in place of ideologies' in *The Infant School : Past, Present and Future* (London: Institute of Education).

Taylor, D. (1983) *Family Literacy: young children learning to read and write* (Exeter N.H.: Heinemann).

Tizard, J. et al (1982) 'Collaboration between teachers and parents in assisting children's reading' *British Journal of Educational Psychology* Vol 52.

Tizard, B. and Hughes, M. (1984) *Young Children Learning: Talking and Thinking at Home and School* (London: Fontana).

Tizard, B., Blatchford, P., Burke, J., Farquahr, C. and Plewis, I. (1988) *Young Children at School in the Inner City* (Hove: Lawrence Erlbaum Associates).

Tough, J. (1977) *Talking and Learning* (London: Ward Lock Educational).

Turner, M. (1990) *Sponsored Reading Failure*.

Varley, B.T. (1992) 'An examination of how Dorothy Heathcote's use of drama can enhance the National Curriculum at Key Stage 2 in the Primary School, both in terms of pupils' learning and as a guide to teachers' presentation, pacing, sequencing and progression of material to be taught.' Unpublished M.A. thesis.

Vygotsky, L. (1962) *Thought and Language* (Cambridge: Mass.: MIT Press).

Vygotsky, L. (1978) *Mind in Society: the development of higher psychological processes* (Cambridge: Harvard University Press).

Wade, B. (1982) 'Reading Rickets and the use of story' *English in Education* **16** (3), 28-37.

Wade, B. (1990) *Reading for Real* (Milton Keynes: Open University Press).

Walkerdine, V. (1983) 'From context to text: a Psychsemiotic approach to abstract thought' in Beveridge, M. *Children thinking about Language* (London: Arnold).

Waterland, L. (1985) *Read with Me: an apprenticeship approach to reading* (Stroud: Signal).

Wells, G. (1981) *Learning through interaction: the study of language development* (Cambridge: Cambridge University Press).

Wells, G. (1987) *The Meaning Makers* (London: Hodder and Stoughton).

Wendon, L. (1986) *First Steps in Letterland* (Barton: Letterland Ltd).

Willinsky, J. (1990) *The new literacy: redefining reading and writing in the schools* (London: Routledge).

Wray, D., Bloom, W. and Hall, N. (1989) *Literacy in Action* (Lewes: Falmer Press).

Index of Authors

170